INDEPENDENCE
OVER
CODEPENDENCY

A SURVIVAL GUIDE TO END TOXIC
RELATIONSHIPS, DEVELOP RADICAL SELF-
LOVE, STOP PEOPLE PLEASING, AND LEARN
HOW TO SET HEALTHY BOUNDARIES FOR
YOUR GROWTH

By
Robert J. Charles, PhD, DMin

Contents

WANT TO OVERCOME OVERTHINKING and MANAGE DIFFICULT PEOPLE?

These **4 FREE** offers are perfect for you: 2 eBooks + 2 audiobooks

In these 2 eBooks + 2 audiobooks, YOU will discover:

- The three different forms of overthinking and how to spot them.
- How ruminating and worrying can damage your social life.
- The types of toxic people and how to escape their web of crises.
- How to discover if you are a highly sensitive person and ways to deal with that.

If you want to finally stop overthinking and being manipulated by others

Get these 4 FREE offers. SCAN with Your Camera

SECOND BONUS

How to Face Any Challenge with Confidence

Download these **FREE 30 BIBLICAL PROMISES** to discover some powerful promises for **YOU**.

At some point, everyone on this Earth faces a tough challenge. Help is on the way! God has your back. His Word will empower you to face any trial or tribulation. These 30 promises from God will give you the strength and resilience you need to move forward.

To get your **FREE** 30 BIBLICAL PROMISES TO OVERCOME ANY CHALLENGE,

SCAN this QR code with Your Camera:

Introduction

Codependency

J essica was a happy young woman who went into marriage with high hopes and expectations. She had dreams and she was ready to make them happen. Her husband seemed like a great catch—just the kind of guy she could build an amazing life with.

So, nothing prepared her for the rude awakening she experienced during her honeymoon: her husband was an alcoholic. Initially, she believed he would get better for her sake. He had to, because she loved him, and she believed he loved her—certainly more than a bottle of beer, right?

Over time, the signs became more difficult to ignore. There was more liquor than love in her house, but she continued to hold on to her dreams of a happy home and a wonderful marriage. At first, it *was easy enough to take care of the house and do everything that needed to be done, including things her husband was responsible for.*

The marriage wasn't getting sour just yet. She could still enjoy a good tangle in the sheets with her husband, even though the fact that he couldn't hold down a job bothered her. Kids were part of her dream marriage, so having them brought no hassle for her. She added caring for them to her list of to-dos.

Unfortunately, the weight of propping up her marriage, parenthood, and running their household soon began to show. She had an essentially irresponsible husband to cater for, she had all the house chores to attend to, and most importantly, she had her kids. She was responsible for everything and everyone, so there was no time left to attend to herself.

Eventually, love turned sour. Care was doled out with obsessive rage. Chores were done in anger. Dreams turned into toxic fantasies. But her husband was to blame for it all!

She hated herself for defending him when she'd first found out he was an alcoholic.

Hate. Bitterness. Rage. Cold responses. These behavioral patterns became her new normal. She got to the point that nothing looked beautiful and rosy to her anymore. The beautiful soul who'd had the strength to fight for her marriage initially had become completely overwhelmed by the tidal waves of negative behavior from her partner. The ugly anger that lay beneath her soul had started manifesting in every part of her life, and it had become so obvious that even her young children could discern, "Mom has gone crazy..."

Why should we care for people so much to the point of getting obsessed with them and unknowingly beginning to control them, manipulate them, get angry at them, and/or become overwhelmed and burned out by the need to take care of them while losing sight of self?

This is a manifestation of what psychologists have identified as codependence. That's not all there is to it, of course; that's why you've got this book in your possession. In this book, you'll learn the rudiments of codependency and how it operates. Have you ever looked at your current or past relationships and wondered why you behaved the way you did? No one sets out to become obsessive when they start to care for someone, but for some of us, it seems like we often find ourselves there, in a state of obsession. So, how did you get there? This book will provide you with that answer.

But just so you know, it's not all your fault. Behaviors don't just happen to people. We inherit a good number of those traits from our parents, and others we learn in childhood, from our peers or authority figures. That's why there's an entire chapter of this book dedicated to the effect your childhood has on your character as a codependent person.

If all this talk about codependence is new to you, and you're thinking that you might be codependent but you aren't sure and/or you don't know what that means—well, you're in the right place. This book will clear up your doubts. I'll share stories of people who were codependent to help you understand what people have been through and how they came out of it. We'll also cover the diverse stances of different psychologists on codependence, and what it actually means to be codependent in a relationship.

This book is also a practical workbook that will help you immensely as a part of your journey to recovery and wholeness. I'll walk you through every inch of the path to recovery; consider me your skillful self-help tour guide. Get your hiking stick ready—you're in for a great journey!

Welcome to your survival guide for ending codependency

PART ONE

Understanding The Situation

One of the greatest benefits of being a human being is the ability to form relationships with others. No matter how great you are as an individual, you'll always need social connection with others. You can see the beauty of these connections in everyday life.

A happy family at the park.

A couple whose love for each other radiates from them.

Kids playing with their beloved dog.

Unfortunately, these connections that make living worthwhile are also one of the easiest aspects of life to turn sour.

Why?

Because in some relationships, the benefits of the relationship aren't mutual. You can think of a relationship where a mother thinks of her children as an extension of herself, and consequently seeks to control every facet of their lives so they can arrive at an outcome she desires. Or think of a situation where a father is living off the kindness of his adult children while he galivants off and lives recklessly. These same negative dynamics can play out in romantic relationships as well, placing a strain on the person who has to sacrifice lots of things, including their happiness, fulfillment, dreams, and aspirations, for the sake of the other person in the relationship.

In this part of the book, we'll focus on two negative kinds of relationships—codependent relationships and narcissistic relationships—that could exist between parent and child or between romantic partners.

We'll also examine how the bond we formed with our parents as children influences our relationships as adults. There's more that we'll dive into as well, but you'll need to see for yourself. Let's jump in!

CHAPTER ONE

How Codependency Works

"Trust in the Lord with all your heart, And lean not on your own understanding."

—Proverbs 3:5 (NKJV)

"A codependent person is one who has let another person's behavior affect him or her, and who is obsessed with controlling that person's behavior."

—Melody Beattie

The Dynamics and Psychology of a Codependent Relationship

Psychologists were the first group of people to stick a label on the trait that Melody Beattie (1992) describes in the quote above, but there's no universal definition for codependency. Different psychologists, authors, and researchers have divergent perspectives on the concept. However, there are a few common traits of codependency that are shared across all definitions.

Jessica, in the story I shared in the introduction to this book, was a codependent person who was affected by the lifestyle of her alcoholic husband. But codependency doesn't always have alcohol in the mix. Let's read about another couple's story.

Ian and Alicia happened to meet and start chatting at the mall and instantly felt a spark. They found out that both of them had just gotten out of toxic relationships, so they could empathize with each other.

They decided to start off as friends, but eventually they inevitably slid into romance. After confessing their feelings for each other, they decided to start a fresh relationship together. Sounds good, right? You'd think that since they were experienced with toxic relationship dynamics, they'd be smart enough to avoid the pitfalls from their previous relationships. But sadly, it didn't work out that way.

They enjoyed the first year of their relationship; then the baggage from their past began to surface. Alicia had a spending issue. Despite her stable, well-paying job, she was often in debt. She tried to conceal the incessant calls from loan companies from Ian, and when they moved in together, she hid the fact that she still owed her old roommates on utility bills.

Let's not forget about Ian here, who in this case became the one going the extra mile to care for his partner while bearing the brunt of the stress alone. When he found out about Alicia's debts, he took it upon himself to pay them off and "fix" her life. Almost as soon as he embarked on that mission, he started feeling the repercussions on his own finances.

He had to delay paying his credit card bills. He couldn't meet his own financial needs because he was scared of declining Alicia's requests for money or assistance with her debts. Ian had a long list of things that bothered him about his girlfriend, but he never seemed to get the chance to sit down with her and talk about them.

Alicia became skillful at guilt tripping him, withholding her love and affection anytime he didn't do exactly what she wanted him to do. Ian was silently suffering; he wasn't comfortable enough with anyone else in his life to unburden himself to them. He secretly wished that Alicia would get a better paying job to sort out her debts, but that remained only a wish.

As though trouble in paradise wasn't enough, Ian was also having trouble at work. He couldn't say no to requests. He routinely worked overtime, and a lot of those hours were spent covering for the professional shortcomings of his colleagues. He worked during Christmas break because his boss demanded that he put in extra hours on an upcoming company project.

Despite knowing he needed time off to recharge, Ian kept going. The demands on his time increased, both by his job and by Alicia. He continually felt pulled in two directions, feeling increasingly angry and clueless about how to sort out his life.

As you can see, neither Alicia nor Ian's work colleagues were drug addicts or alcoholics, yet Ian is still demonstrating codependent behavior. His life ended up at the same climax of every codependent tale—bitterness and anger, where the rottenness beneath the once-beautiful soul begins to emerge, and the codependent becomes resentful and enraged by everything that happens to them. Their capacity to love and be good to others while neglecting themselves becomes overstretched, and their only response is an ugly outburst.

So, now that we've seen two examples, what does codependency mean?

Codependence isn't exactly a word you hear every day. Let's first try to understand where the word comes from.

A closer look at the word "codependence" reveals that it's formed from the combination of the prefix "co" and the word "dependence." *Dependence* is a common word; as you probably know, if you are dependent on someone or something, it means you can't do without them, right?

Co is a prefix that means "together" or "mutual."

In other words, codependents are *mutually dependent* on each other.

Is it bad to be mutually dependent? After all, most couples are mutually dependent, aren't they? Even colleagues at work can be mutually dependent on each other to get things done, right? It's true—none of us can really do anything all alone. As we mentioned in the introduction to this part of the book, we are social creatures and we rely on our relationships with others.

However, there is a version of mutual dependence that can become very unhealthy, and that's what codependence is.

Now let's take a look at some signs of codependence.

Am I Codependent?

Before we look at the symptoms of codependence, let's dive into another story.

Gerald was a handsome man in his forties. He was a successful businessman, but couldn't transmit that skill into keeping his romantic relationships with women alive. His first marriage of 13 years ended in a messy divorce. He mourned his dead marriage for two months, then fell in love again. She was an alcoholic just like his first wife. He spent months trying to help her out of her addiction, but he ended up hurting himself. Instead of getting help for his partner, he became resentful because every attempt proved fruitless. She wouldn't stop drinking. Gerald was devastated and eventually ended the relationship.

A hopeless romantic, Gerald fell in love with another woman shortly after, and guess what? She was also an alcoholic. Gerald hadn't given himself time to recover from his past woes. He was in shambles himself, yet he kept throwing himself into new relationships and bearing the burdens of others.

Like Jessica, who we talked about in the introduction, Gerald remained willfully blind to his new girlfriend's problems. He defended her. He lied to himself that she wasn't the problem—he was. He tried to enjoy his relationship with her, but it only got uglier.

After a while, he felt he needed help and he went to see a counselor. After a few sessions, the therapist suggested that Gerald's problem was rooted in his family, because his father and older brother were alcoholics, and having to take care of them had affected him deeply.

The therapist brought up the idea that he might be codependent, but Gerald rejected the diagnosis and concluded that nothing was wrong with the women he had dated. Attributing the failures to simple bad luck, he hoped his luck would turn and threw himself fully into dating once more. This should not be surprising, as self-denial is a key trait of codependency (Elder, 2018).

Our focus in reading this story should not be on judging Gerald's situation. Rather, the point is to understand that you don't have to linger in a state of self-denial that leads you into the depths of pain and resentment before you come to the truth.

The following signs will help you figure out if you're codependent or not. Circle the appropriate answer after each statement.

- You're obsessed with taking care of other person's needs. **yes / no**

- You perceive yourself as completely unselfish and dedicated to the wellbeing of others. **yes / no**
- You judge what you think, say, or do as never good enough. **yes / no**
- You're embarrassed to receive recognition, praise, or gifts. **yes / no**
- You have a hard time with self-acceptance. **yes / no**
- You find it difficult to make decisions in a relationship. **yes / no**
- You keep redefining your personal boundaries to accommodate other people. **yes / no**
- You find it difficult to express your needs in a relationship. **yes / no**
- You're quick to say yes to your partner's every wish without considering the effect on you. **yes / no**
- You always make excuses for your partner's bad behavior. **yes / no**
- You've lost your sense of identity, interests, and desires. **yes / no**
- You give more to your partner than you're getting back. **yes / no**
- You become resentful when your partner declines your help or rejects your advice. **yes / no**

- You lack trust in yourself and have poor self-esteem. **yes / no**

- You're afraid of being abandoned. **yes / no**

- You depend on unhealthy people in relationships, to your own detriment. **yes / no**

- You magnify your sense of responsibility for the actions of others. **yes / no**

- Your relationships are built on conditional, controlling, and coercive behaviors. **yes / no**

- You use indirect or evasive language to avoid conflict. **yes / no**

- You believe that displaying emotion is a sign of weakness. **yes / no**

The list above isn't exhaustive; however, with that list, you should be able to establish which side of the codependent coin you're on. But there's still more you need to learn about this pattern.

Codependency in Families

A family unit is one of the relationship contexts in which codependence can be experienced. Most times this happens between parents and children. According to Lewis (2020), one of the ways to identify codependents in a family is when a parent has an unhealthy attachment to their child, going overboard to exercise excessive control over the child's life because of that attachment.

Lewis (2020) explains that, for example, a codependent parent may expect their child to keep them mentally stable and emotionally happy, essentially viewing the child as responsible for their wellbeing. Furthermore, if this behavior is perpetuated for a long enough time, it will lead to chaos and throw the family into a dark spiral of resentment and dissatisfaction.

From another perspective, when a family member struggles with addiction of any kind, it can prevent others within the family from living their own lives happily. It's not difficult to see why; our natural response is to help our family members however we can—and that's a great intention. But, as great as that is, it could also create a codependent relationship that will hurt other members of the family, and might eventually hamper the recovery of that loved one from the addictive situation.

Being emotionally connected to problems in the lives of other people can make us lose our identity, self-worth, beautiful soul, integrity, happiness, serenity, and individuality. We'll begin to compromise our boundaries and value system just to help the other person.

If you find that you constantly feel the need to save someone in your family who has a destructive behavioral pattern, or you feel drawn to someone who is struggling emotionally or physically and constantly put their needs before yours, you're tilting towards codependence.

But shouldn't you help people with such issues in your family? Quite frankly—no! Does that answer surprise you? This book isn't an advocate of selfishness or cruelty by any means. You have the liberty to help others, but your decisions shouldn't lead to severe behavioral patterns that cause you to unintentionally endorse the addictive or toxic behaviors of your family member, or lead you to go out of your way to meet their physical or emotional needs while you get lost in the midst of that genuine effort. Your beautiful soul might end up turning sour and resentful when everything that you loved about the other person begins to be darkened.

Either of your parents could be physically or emotionally attached to you in an unhealthy way, and this could make them develop obsessive behavioral patterns.

One final note: This could also be generational. Maybe you were the child of a codependent parent growing up, and now you're a parent and you're witnessing the same obsessive behavioral pattern towards your child in yourself. The things I'll share in this chapter will be helpful to you.

The Codependent Mother

Mothers are amazing caregivers, but sometimes they overdo it. And when they do, it strains their relationship with their children. Carter (2022) shares some real-life comments from mothers who unintentionally found themselves in the codependence conundrum. This could be you, too:

> *"My aha moment came when I paid 3 months of my 21-year-old son's rent (and skipped a mortgage payment of my own) because it's easier knowing his housing is secure than to properly and formally put boundaries in place that may require immediate investment and change from him."* – *@elle_acha*

> *"One of my kids would get angry/frustrated when I asked him to do chores or follow through on things when he was little. I did a lot for him growing up. Summer before he left for college, he told me he was super worried because he didn't know how to do a lot of things for himself—like laundry, cook, make a doctor's appointment. And of course, this was my fault. I was protecting him and myself and took away the opportunity for him to feel self-sufficient and feel like he can take care of himself."* – *Anonymous*

Dr. Ashurina Ream, a clinical psychologist, notes that codependency in mothers (or parents generally) "creates worry and internal pressure to be others-focused" (as cited by Carter, 2022).

Mothers should be part of their child's growth up to a certain stage of life. They are often so connected to their child that they know what the child is feeling or thinking. This is a great quality for a mom to have—and if you're reading this and you're a mother, you might notice this trait in yourself. But where the strain starts is when your child grows older and yet you still feel you have the same role as you did when your child was just a toddler. Once your child matures and becomes a teenager or young adult, you cannot continue to make certain decisions for them. You must realize at some point that you're not meant to tell them what to do all their lives. They'll rebel one day. Nobody likes to be controlled or to have decisions made for them.

As a mother, when you begin to overdo what you perceive to be your God-given responsibility to your children, you may also begin to lose your relationship with your partner. You'll be so focused on tending to the needs of your child (or children) that you cease to see your partner. Your romantic relationship begins to wane because you have a new priority. Additionally, out of fear of what might happen to your child if you don't do what you feel you need to do, you begin to take less care of yourself than you should. You become so attached that you no longer know the line that separates caregiving from codependency.

These are further signs that indicate you're a codependent mother. Remember to circle yes or no so you can easily track your answers.

- You find yourself fighting to control your child's behavior. **yes/no**

- You try to rescue your child from painful emotional experiences. **yes/no**

- You excessively feel the need to create a perfect world for your child. **yes/no**

- You sacrifice your romantic relationship with your partner to focus on your child. **yes/no**

- Your self-esteem is tied to your relationship with your child and their feelings, behavior, wellbeing, etc. **yes/no**

- You have a difficult time enforcing boundaries because you're afraid your child will become hostile towards you. **yes/no**

- You invest so much in your child that you gradually lose sight of yourself and abandon your own interests. **yes/no**

- You depend on your child for emotional support, which you might not always get. **yes/no**

If you've been exhibiting any of these behavioral patterns as a mother, don't panic. I know you didn't mean to go to the extreme. I understand that you want the best for your child, and that's what every good and caring mother should want. Being a codependent mother doesn't make you a bad mom; it's only an indication that you've overdone certain things, and you can rectify them.

Your child might have misinterpreted your acts of love as something else, but that's okay. You don't need to become more anxious, resentful, or hostile. Focus on channeling the same energy you've been using to release negative vibes around your home towards loving yourself and paying more attention to your own needs.

The Codependent Father

Fathers represent many things in their homes. In an ideal family setting, a father is the primary caretaker of the family. He is always around to provide support and to guide his children. He stays close behind them to catch them if they fall, both physically and metaphorically.

But you know that when we dote on people, we tend to overdo it sometimes. We may unintentionally hurt the people we dote on, or even ourselves. Just like mothers, fathers can also carry out their parental duties so excessively that they become overly attached to their child. Don't view executing your duties as a father as all there is to your life. If you feel that doing the things you do for your children is your only way to gain a sense of fulfillment, you're a codependent father.

Look, you're right to love your children. You're right to support them. You're right to stand by them. Those are amazing responsibilities that make you an amazing dad. But the moment you begin to feel you need to put more energy into carrying out your parental duties than into caring for yourself and your partner, you need to check yourself. When you start feeling you need to go out of your way to control the lives of your children and guard them from harm, then you're already beginning to slide towards codependency.

If you continue to adopt this kind of mindset, you'll no longer see yourself as a priority. You'll work and toil just to make your children happy while depriving yourself of rest and happiness. This mindset will also cause you to forget that you met your partner before you met your kids, and your romantic relationship will begin to decline. Pull yourself out of self-denial. Your identity is more than just a father.

Codependency in Romantic Relationships: What it Looks Like

I've already given you practical examples of codependency in romantic relationships. Jessica was the first example, and Gerald was another. The common thread between the two stories was the trait of self-denial. At some point in their relationships, they were under the illusion that their self-worth and actualization came from their responses to the needs of their partner. But their partners kept taking advantage of their vulnerability.

They felt guilty for not meeting their partner's needs, even if it meant neglecting their own needs. They sacrificed their aspirations on the altar of their partner's extravagance. They suffered loss of identity. They became resentful. They became hostile.

That's because what keeps relationships going for a long period of time isn't becoming the sacrificial lamb who gains nothing while losing their voice, self-worth, power, and identity. Relationships work well when partners understand the balance of meeting each other's needs without incessantly sacrificing for the other person. That balance is the ideal for any relationship.

According to Sanam Hafeez, a neuropsychologist and professor at Columbia University, (as cited by Santilli et.al, 2022), codependency in romantic relationships usually ensues from the parent-child relationship. Hafeez (2022) notes that codependent romantic relationships tend to form more often when people have had toxic relationships with a parent or other family member in the past.

But even if you are simply a naturally selfless and devoted giver in romantic relationships, with no history of codependency, you can still become codependent. To be a devoted giver isn't a bad thing, of course; it's one of the most beautiful characteristics of a beautiful soul. But if your need to give is wrapped in a need to be needed while you're excessively meeting the needs of your partner and neglecting your own, you've become codependent. And that relationship is unhealthy.

If you feel the need to apologize for everything, even for what your partner did wrong, that's another sign you could be codependent. This could be done because you're scared to offend your partner or you want to keep the peace in the relationship. There's nothing healthy about a relationship where one partner begins to feed off the other. Trying to keep such a relationship alive makes you a codependent person who's deluded by self-deceit.

Why You Need to Stop Codependency

Codependency in any form of relationship is really toxic. While the codependent is trying to put everything into the relationship, the enabler (the other person, for whom the codependent is giving their all) gives nothing or very little of themselves. This type of relationship is harmful for both parties, but is especially dangerous for the codependent individual.

You have a life to live. You have dreams to pursue. You have a purpose on Planet Earth to fulfill. Being codependent will hamper all these things. If you don't want to remain under the self-deceptive illusion that Gerald was under in one of the stories I shared, you'll need to jolt yourself back to reality. It's not bad luck that put you in the codependent family or romantic relationship you're in. Don't become hostile to God. The choice to be all you've been created to be lies with you.

You can work on yourself if you've been exhibiting the signs of codependency as listed in this book. Later on, I'll show you some steps to help you stop being codependent—don't be complacent about following them. Let's get to work to get you living independently of anyone or anything.

Workbook One

Exercise One: Understanding Your Situation

This workbook will focus on helping to ascertain whether you're codependent or not. You have to recognize some of the signs that come with codependency.

Tick either yes or no.

NUMBER	QUESTION	YES	NO
1.	Are you obsessed with taking care of people's needs?		
2.	Do you neglect your own needs?		
3.	Do you ALWAYS (or 90% of the time) make excuses for people's actions?		
4.	Are you vulnerable to people's emotions?		
5.	Do you have a sense of fulfillment when you provide for people?		
6.	Is it challenging to say no to people's requests?		

7.	Is it difficult for you to talk about your needs or burden?		
8.	Do you like controlling people?		
9.	Do you trust yourself?		
10.	Are you always happy when working for people?		
11.	Do you doubt your decisions oftentimes?		
12.	Do you feel guilty when doing something for yourself?		
13.	Do people's moods affect your personality?		
14.	Do you always apologize for everything?		

If you answered YES to all or most of the above questions, then you are codependent.

Exercise Two: How Do You See Yourself?

At the core of codependency is someone who has lost so much faith in himself or herself that they view other people as more important than they are. This exercise is focused on helping you track your inner beliefs to see what damaging thoughts you might be harboring about yourself that may be fueling your codependency habits.

Examining My Self-beliefs

True or False Statements

Read each statement and write if it is true or false about
your inner thoughts

1. I don't see myself as important.   _____

2. People should make
   sacrifices for me   _____

3. It's not easy to love someone
   like me   _____

4. I'm happy even if others
   aren't   _____

5. I'm beautiful and valued   _____

6. I'll only be happy when my
   family is happy   _____

7. I'm ready to sacrifice
   everything, even myself   _____

8. I need to focus all my attention on protecting my loved ones

_____

9. I deserve all the happiness that this world can give

_____

10. Sometimes, I'm just a waste of space

_____

11. God must hate me

_____

12. My life is worth nothing if my loved ones aren't happy and satisfied

_____

13. I'm valuable

_____

14. I shouldn't be unhappy because I want to make others happy

_____

From your answers, you'll be able to see for yourself the extent of the self-damaging thoughts that you've been harboring.

Chapter One Takeaway

Codependency is a serious problem that eats up many relationships that otherwise would have been great. The first step to thrashing out this issue is checking for sure signs that you're codependent. When you realize that you need help, half of the problem is solved.

CHAPTER TWO

The Impact Of Childhood Experiences And Attachment Styles

"Fathers, do not provoke your children, lest they become discouraged."

—Colossians 3:21 (NKJV)

"All hurt is founded on attachment to anything regardless of its nature. When we detach we vibrationally send ourselves back into the flow of life."

—Dr. Jacinta Mpalyenkana, Ph.D., MBA

Does Childhood Impact Codependency?

Just like many other psychological traits, positive or negative, codependence may be rooted in childhood experiences. Most children form the basis for future relationships through their relationship with their parents. Does that apply to you?

I invite you to test this briefly. Reflect on how your relationship with your parents and other members of your family has shaped your present relationships with people.

What did you discover?

One of the things I've learned about codependency is that any child who was raised by over- or under-protective parents has a higher chance of developing codependency issues.

If you were raised by an overprotective parent, you'll remember that they shielded you from anything or anyone they perceived as a threat. That sounds good, right? But what does that loving act do to one's mental state? It takes from you the confidence to face your own threats when your parents aren't there to protect you anymore. Instead of growing a lion heart, as an adult you end up running away when confronted by situations that your parents used to protect you from.

You'll grow scared of ever stepping out to try new things because you were shielded from facing challenges or tough things as a child.

For example, your parents may have prevented you, out of pure love, from learning to ride a bicycle because they feared you would break a bone. Doesn't that sound logical? But it can only be logical up to a point in your period of development as a child. If such overprotectiveness continues as the child grows older, it creates negative psychological consequences that will influence the child's future relationships, leading to codependence on other people and making fear the basis of critical decisions.

Consider another scenario. If, in your childhood, your parents pampered you so much you couldn't acquire the basic life skills you need to survive as an independent adult, you'll always be looking for someone to fulfill those needs for you.

The reason there is an astounding number of freshman college students who have no basic household cleaning skills is due to this unhealthy type of parenting. Whatever motivated the parents to not let their child learn these skills, it isn't good for the mental formation of the child. When they become adults, they'll always feel entitled to be served and expect other people to do things for them while they enjoy a luxurious life without caring how those things get done.

This style of parenting is one of the things Amy Mitchell, in the 2016 American comedy *Bad Moms*, fights against. She takes on the responsibility of doing virtually everything around the house, including driving her two kids to school. Her husband does next to nothing at home, and her kids think they're entitled to having everything done for them, including their school assignments. Amy becomes stressed and starts to revolt against the school system that makes moms do virtually everything for their children.

She succeeds. The result? Her son starts taking responsibility for his homework. He doesn't wait for her to serve him breakfast before going to school.

Unfortunately, one of the reasons there are lots of codependents in our society today is because they were raised with this entitled mentality.

Okay, so we know lots of parents are overprotective. How do parents under-protect their children? This is the flip side of the overprotective coin. While overprotective parents give their children everything they need and more, under-protective parents do the exact opposite. They don't provide enough support for their child during their different developmental stages. This leaves the child vulnerable; the child will grow up feeling insecure and lonely and become an adult who feels less deserving of any form of love. It breeds low self-worth, low self-esteem, and low self-love.

From my own study and observation, I've seen lots of children who were raised by parents who had substance use issues as well. These children have a greater tendency towards codependency too. In this context, the child becomes the caregiver while their parent becomes the receiver. That's an unhealthy kind of relationship, and it's against the natural order. When children find themselves in such a situation, they learn to neglect their own needs to meet the needs of the parent or family member. They'll grow up feeling responsible for everyone around them, but not themselves.

People who experience this will, most times, derive happiness from other people's satisfaction—that is, they will only have a sense of satisfaction after they've met the needs of people around them.

Which side of the coin do you belong to? Have you been raised by overprotective parents or under-protective parents?

The Different Attachment Theories

Attachment theory was first propounded by two psychologists, John Bowlby and, later, Mary Ainsworth, in the 1960s and 1970s respectively. According to them (as cited by Gonsalves, 2022), people's attachment styles are shaped and developed in their early childhood. And this happens in response to their relationships with their earliest caregivers.

According to Mancao (as cited by Gonsalves, 2022), the spectrum of our attachment style ranges from how we respond emotionally to others to how we interact with our partner in relationships to how we behave generally in relationships.

The chart below is a depiction of how the four attachment styles are measured on the basis of an individual's degree of avoidance and anxiety in relationship:

Avoidant	Fearful-Avoidant
Secure	Anxious

Parents (especially moms) are often the first caregivers that children meet upon their arrival on Earth. Although parents' roles are numerous, they have one important one in the midst of the many: just being there.

The influence parents have on children through their presence cannot be overemphasized. A parent's presence makes a child feel loved and secure. Just being there is what also produces attachment.

As portrayed in the chart above, there are four basic types of attachment:

- Secure attachment
- Anxious-insecure attachment
- Avoidant-insecure attachment

- Fearful-avoidant attachment (also known as disorganized-insecure attachment)

Let's examine each of these attachment styles in greater detail.

Secure Attachment

This is the best identified form of attachment. It's an attachment that forms a secure and loving relationship with other people. This kind of attachment is formed when parents or caregivers are available, sensitive, accepting, and responsive.

Parents who form a secure attachment with their children allow them the freedom to spend time with their friends and with other kids in the community. But they also wait for their children to come back to hear about how they spent their day and to comfort them during hard times if the need arises.

One of the processes that also leads to the formation of this attachment style is when parents learn to have fun with their children. Through play and fun activities, the child learns to express positive and negative emotions and receives the right responses from the parent. Children who develop a secure attachment style don't have issues trusting people. They have a good sense of self-worth and self-esteem. They don't doubt what they're capable of doing. These are the kinds of children who grow up into well-rounded adults and go on to have healthy relationships.

That's what we're aiming for!

Trust, love, and acceptance are common traits for securely attached people. They feel sufficient in themselves and they don't feel their happiness in life is dependent on their partner.

Anxious-Insecure Attachment

What do you think an anxious attachment will produce? That's right—fear. There's no way an anxious attachment can be secure. It's an insecure attachment style that is laced with fear of abandonment.

This attachment style is formed when parents are not always available to attend to the needs of their child. Since the parents are distant, either physically or emotionally, the child cannot trust the parents to be around when needed. Therefore, the child has no guarantee of security coming from the attachment figure. The result is that the child will be afraid to explore since there's no guarantee of safety from the parent.

The child will sometimes activate a distress mode, hoping this will compel their parent to respond. The child will also become needy and resentful. When these people grow into adults, they're unlikely to feel secure in their relationships. They'll be afraid that their partner might abandon them in the same way their parents usually did. Thus, they'll desperately seek reassurance and validation from their partner.

Avoidant-Insecure Attachment

This attachment style is a bit different from the anxious attachment style. Even children are aware when their parents are trying to avoid them, and it creates an insecure attachment. For whatever reason, some parents might find it difficult to accept or respond sensitively to the needs of their child.

For example, when the parent refuses to comfort the child when needed, but instead chooses to reject and reduce the child's feelings, it can produce an avoidant-insecure attachment. The parent may also refuse to assist with difficult tasks. The child will then begin to consider the parent nonexistent since the parent refuses to respond when needed.

The child is thus trained from that tender stage to lock up their feelings and not expect anything from anyone. They feel there's no point in expressing emotions since they have no one to share them with. Such children grow up to be adults who are not moved to tears by sad or touching events, and even when they feel pain, they refuse to show it.

They grow up believing that nothing good can come from relationships, and therefore, there's no need to trust anyone. These kinds of people prefer to be independent and consider romantic relationships stressful. If they are in a relationship, they try to maintain emotional distance from their partner.

Fearful-Avoidant (Disorganized-Insecure) Attachment

This is the worst form of attachment and the most hazardous for any relationship. In many cases, you won't want to share the same room with people who grew up with this form of attachment. It's almost certain the relationship will be toxic and not produce anything good—at least, not unless some serious steps are taken.

I say all that because children who have formed a fearful-avoidant attachment style with their parents were rejected, ridiculed, and frightened by their parents. Parents that display this kind of hostility towards their children are often those who have an ugly past themselves, such as some form of trauma. Unfortunately, the only thing such parents can give to their child is negativity, instilling fear and insecurity in the child.

This final attachment style is also known as disorganized-insecure because, unlike the first three attachment styles where the child is organized and consistent in their behavioral pattern, the child's strategy here is disorganized and inconsistent. This also influences the child's behavioral pattern. In order to feel safe apart from their parents, children who form this attachment style become aggressive in adult relationships, refuse to care for others, and are entirely self-reliant.

This attachment style is rare, but unfortunately, many people who form this type of attachment in childhood will grow into violent partners.

Identifying Your Attachment Style

Each of us was raised in different contexts by different parents. Our behavioral patterns in our relationships with others are partly due to the attachment style we formed with our parents in our childhood. That means that there's a link between your relationships as an adult and the type of relationship you had with your parents during your childhood.

John Bowlby, a British developmental psychologist and psychiatrist, wrote a lot about attachment theory. He showed how each attachment style begins to come together from as early as infanthood.

The following are signs of each type of attachment in adults so that you can assess your attachment style.

Secure Attachment

People with this attachment style:

- Have high self-esteem
- Can control their emotions
- Have no issues trusting other people
- Have great communication skills
- Can seek emotional support
- Feel comfortable being alone
- Have good conflict management skills
- Are comfortable in close relationships

- Are able to self-reflect in relationships
- Are easy to connect with
- Manage conflict well
- Are emotionally available
- Are not scared to share feelings with partners and friends

Anxious Attachment

People with this attachment style:

- Are sensitive to criticism
- Are often clingy and/or jealous
- Are afraid of being alone
- Suffer from low self-esteem
- Feel unworthy of love
- Have a fear of rejection
- Have a fear of abandonment
- Can't trust others easily

Avoidant Attachment

People with this attachment style:

- Have issues with intimacy
- Are almost emotionless in social and romantic relationships

- Are unwilling to share their thoughts or feelings with others
- Avoid emotional intimacy
- Avoid physical intimacy
- Have a sense of independence
- Have difficulty trusting people
- Feel threatened by anyone who tries to get close
- Enjoy being alone
- See no need to have others around them

Fearful-Avoidant Attachment

This attachment style creates:

- Contrasting behavioral patterns
- Fear of rejection
- Unstable emotions
- Anxiety
- Inability to trust people

You can test where you belong on the attachment style chart by paying attention to these signs in your own behavior. Whatever you find out, especially if you turn out to have an insecure attachment, it's just an indication of your current state. It doesn't imply you'll be tied to that style forever. In fact, that's why you have this book in your hands: you can form a new, healthy attachment style because you have the capacity to change and form new behavioral patterns.

How Your Attachment Style Is Formed

How did your attachment style develop? Most attachments develop at a very tender age. Mental health counselor Grace Suh (as cited by Gonsalves, 2022) says that the relationship parents develop with their children in the first 11 months of existence is paramount in the formation of the child's attachment style.

If you've been paying attention to the last few sections, you should have realized by now that it's not entirely your fault that you behave the way you do. Because, really, what could you possibly have done to change something for yourself when you were just 11 months old? Your behavioral formation is first dependent on your parents or primary caregivers.

Generally, even though babies can't speak, they still have a mode of communication with their parents. Attachment is formed based on the parents' response to that communication. If you're a parent, keep in mind that your responses to your baby in the first few months of life will shape what becomes the bedrock of their future relationships.

What kind of responses lead to the development of each attachment style?

Secure Attachment

Responses:

Consistent availability and being sensitive to needs.

You felt safe and secure in childhood because your parents were always there for you. You got reassurance from your parents for certain actions, comfort when you were hurt, and loving discipline when you erred.

This response builds up to make you feel valued, loved, safe, and understood in your early interactions with your parents.

The responses you got from your parents at that stage of your life indicate that your parents were emotionally stable themselves.

Anxious Attachment

Responses:

Inconsistent availability, unpredictable affection, and occasional withdrawal.

This response instills fear, especially fear of being abandoned, in children. If in your childhood your parents were not always available to attend to your needs or comfort you when needed, you'll likely grow up into an adult who's scared of trusting people you're in a relationship with.

You'll look for constant reassurance from your partner that you're still needed in the relationship.

Avoidant Attachment

Responses:

Dismissive and distant. Disconnected from the needs of the child.

This kind of response leads the child to believe that nothing valuable could come to them from relationships; thus, they grow up with the mentality of being self-reliant, and they avoid any form of emotional expression.

They view relationships as burdensome and, if they are in a relationship, try to avoid meaningful conversations or maintain emotional distance from their partner.

Fearful-Avoidant (Disorganized) Attachment

Responses:

Outright neglect and/or abuse. Frightening and traumatizing.

This attachment style is the most extreme of all four styles. Here, the child has no sense of what a healthy relationship looks like. It's difficult for people in this category to trust people in relationships. Their behavioral pattern is usually disorganized because their parents were a source of both comfort and fear.

Changing an Unhealthy Attachment Style

In a personal blog, Seth Blais (2020) shares his personal story of traumatic experiences during childhood. Those experiences shaped his adulthood, especially his relationships with people. The attachment he formed with his parents was the extreme one: fearful-avoidant or disorganized attachment. As a boy, he became acquainted with violence as a rite of passage, a critical event in his childhood experience. He grew up in a dysfunctional family under the rule of an abusive and emotionally unavailable father who had his own problems to deal with. Seth's emotional needs were unintentionally neglected, and therefore he grew up with feelings of abandonment and fears that his future romantic relationships would have the same outcome.

His story is a rare case of fearful-avoidant attachment. Can such people be helped? Yes! It's possible to change an unhealthy attachment style as an adult—unless you want to remain as you are, that is, doling out negativity to the people around you.

Here comes the golden question: "How can I change my unhealthy attachment style?"

1. Recognize and Admit

The first step to changing an unhealthy attachment is to be sincere with *yourself* to recognize that the attachment you formed with your parents as a child could be responsible for your current relationship woes. Essentially, you must admit that the relationship you had with your parents or primary caregiver as a child has shaped (or is still shaping) your present-day relationships.

To do this is to take the first and most critical step toward liberation—liberation from the influence of unhealthy childhood experiences on your adult life.

2. Be Willing to Change

Bowlby, the first psychologist to promulgate attachment theory, didn't believe we could change our attachment style. However, advanced studies in neuroscience have proven that people can indeed change the way their brain works.

But you know how these things are; change doesn't come served to you on a golden platter. Rewiring the brain to work differently from how it's been used to working over many years is extremely difficult—almost impossible. However, it can be done. The key factor that will help you stay in the process of transformation is your willingness to make the change.

Sure, you might want a change in your behavioral pattern... but are you willing to put in the work to make that change happen?

3. Raise Your Self-Esteem

Each form of insecure and unhealthy attachment dampens your self-esteem. At the extreme of the attachment spectrum is a battered self-esteem. However, irrespective of the level of damage, your self-esteem can be recovered.

Although you may have been raised in an atmosphere that took your self-esteem from you, you can create an atmosphere that lets you see how valuable and lovable you are. Be assured that you're not a bad person. You only grew up in a toxic relationship, which taught you that you're less deserving of love and attention. But that's a lie. You deserve all the love in the world. And you deserve to be listened to. Your needs are valid.

Raise your self-esteem with the truth about *you* that I just shared. It'll take you further in changing your unhealthy attachment style.

4. Confront the Real Need

Insecure attachment styles develop due to how our parents responded to our needs. As adults, when we allow that style to linger in our relationships with people, the real underlying issue is that we still have needs, but we feel that if we share those needs with our partner, we'll get the same response we got from our parents in childhood. Thus, we sometimes choose not to express our needs for fear of re-experiencing what happened in the past.

Securely attached people have healthy relationships because they know how to express their needs. Thus, if you want to enjoy good relationships with people, learn to express your needs sincerely.

Childhood experiences are life-shapers, both positive and negative. But the good news is that as adults, we can fix whatever was broken during our childhood. If having a great life of self-actualization and purposeful accomplishment is your goal, committing *yourself* to change is a worthy effort.

Workbook Two

Exercise One

Circle and write your answers.

- Do you think your parents were overprotective? YES / NO

- Write down four things you wish you had done during childhood that your parents didn't permit.

1. _____

2. _____

3. _____

4. _____

- How did not doing those things affect you?

_____

_____

_____

_____

- Do you think your parents were under-protective? YES / NO

- Write down four things your parents were supposed to do for you that you had to do by yourself.

1. _____

2. _____

3. _____

4. _____

Exercise Two

In light of the discussion about attachment styles, which of the four styles do you belong to, and why do you think this is the style that best describes you?

_____

_____

_____

_____

_____

Do you like the attachment style that you have?

_____

_____

How has this style affected you (whether positively or negatively) in times past?

_____

_____

_____

_____

Chapter Two Takeaway

Your attachment style is intricately linked to the issues you are having now with codependency. It's important to identify your attachment style in order to arm yourself with more useful information as you proceed on this healing journey. Feel free to go back into the exercises to be sure that you've identified your attachment style correctly. Now it's time to take a look at something else that's closely linked to codependency: narcissism.

CHAPTER THREE

Codependency and Narcissism

"Before destruction the heart of a man is haughty, and before honor is humility."

—Proverbs 18:12 (NKJV)

"To a narcissist they always take the lead, they want to dominate the conversation and make things about themselves. Their sense of importance makes them think that as their partner, you are there to serve them..."

—Courtney Evans

The Relationship between Codependency and Narcissism

Naina didn't know what narcissism was until she had a firsthand experience in the space of 12 months.

She was introduced to the "love of her life," Jeff, through a family friend. They got off to a great start; the young man seemed like a great, kind, and respectable person. Early in their dating relationship, he showered her with gifts and affection, like she was all that mattered to him. They went on extravagant and romantic dates. Their relationship blossomed, or so it seemed. She thought that if she could marry such an amazing man, it would be happily ever after.

They got engaged in a matter of weeks. That was when it dawned on Naina what kind of man she had tied the knot with and things began to sour. However, she tried to shut her eyes to the slight changes she noticed in him. The changes in his character had begun to unfold in the weeks leading up to their marriage, but she had always defended him. They'd fought and disagreed over issues before marriage, but she'd decided to let them slide each time.

To keep the marriage alive, Naina allowed Jeff to control her in every way he wanted. She sheepishly did whatever he told her to do. Despite this, her husband cheated on her, and her in-laws were as cruel and aggressive towards her as the lord of hell himself. They rejected her, and they made it clear. Naina was gaslighted, restricted from visiting her family or friends, verbally abused, and ridiculed until she mustered the strength to walk away from the marriage.

Naina's husband is just one of many narcissists walking the streets of our communities. You might have met one yourself. And if you have, you might have seen a glimpse of what it means to live with one. When you live with one, you're basically living in a state of confusion.

The word "narcissism" is used in different contexts today, but it has a specific connotation in psychology. Narcissism is not an appreciation of self in the genuine sense. People with narcissistic personality have an idealized image of themselves. They're in love with this magnified self-image. They only feel uneasy whenever their narcissistic confidence is threatened. This tendency makes people with narcissistic personality take others for granted or exploit them. People with this personality are not just hostile to the people around them, but they also don't feel or understand the effect of their behavior on other people.

Narcissism is a personality trait, but it is also a personality disorder. Not everyone who has a narcissistic tendency has narcissistic personality disorder (NPD); people at the lower end of the narcissist spectrum only exhibit some of its traits. It's those at the highest point of the spectrum that fall into the NPD category.

Just like Naina's husband, narcissists are often charming and confident. At the outset of their relationships, they don't usually show any negative tendency right away. At that stage it's difficult to know their true nature.

Narcissism vs. Codependence

Narcissism and codependency are similar in that they are connected to a distorted view of self. Both categories of people place a lot of importance on what people think about them. To get a sense of their self-worth, they need people. The only difference is that their method of getting validation from people differs.

Narcissists have an excessive focus on themselves. Everything in the room must be about them, and if that doesn't happen, they explode. And when they do explode, they don't care what effect it has on other people.

Narcissists always need people's affection and admiration to feel good about themselves.

On the other hand, codependents are often excessively focused on others. In their distorted perspective of themselves, their essence, relevance, and esteem come from meeting the needs of other people. In their zeal to serve others, they may assume control and dominance over the person they're trying to help because they perceive that what they're doing for the person is what's best for them.

Unlike narcissists, they don't need people to magnify their image; they just want to feel needed.

One other similarity between the two personality traits is that both are excessive in their expressions.

Signs That You're Being Abused by a Narcissist

The signs that point to the fact that you're in a toxic relationship with a narcissist are usually accompanied by some excessive negativity. Merciless violation of boundaries, manipulation, and demeaning treatment that make you lose your sense of self-worth are all signs that you're in a relationship with a narcissist.

Also, when you feel like you no longer know yourself, and you've been so devalued that you feel worthless, know that you're almost certainly being abused by a narcissist.

Other signs include:

1. Broken hedge

Narcissists enjoy breaking through the "hedge" of their victims. Thus, their victims are handicapped—their power to make independent choices is taken away from them. Some victims have reported that they no longer have me-time or security because their arrogant abuser takes the liberty of going through their personal stuff, including their personal journal or private emails.

It can get so bad that the victim can't make independent decisions about their own body. Their body is cruelly violated, and its care is at the beck and call of their abuser. If this is you, your partner is a narcissist.

2. Aggressive threats of physical violence

Narcissistic abusers are obnoxious con artists who focus on emotional manipulation. They can achieve this through different vicious acts, including violent outbursts, self-harm, and other scary episodes. They crave attention and will do whatever they deem necessary in their distorted mind to achieve it.

3. Verbal abuse

Does your partner derive joy and self-satisfaction from insulting you till you don't trust your personal judgment? Your partner is probably a narcissist. Verbal abuse is one of the tools at the disposal of narcissists, used to belittle their partner. They may even make a joke of the verbal abuse or say things subtly, but it's always done to degrade the victim.

4. Public destruction of image

Narcissists are also good at manipulating their partners by lying about them to trusted loved ones. With that, their victims are at their mercy. They distort valuable information about their partners and share it with those whom their victims esteem highly. This ruins the public image or social standing of the victimized.

5. Overwhelming self-doubt

When you're in a relationship with a narcissist, one of the telling signs is that you'll begin to doubt yourself. The battering, blaming, and accusations from your partner will make you feel uncertain about things, including yourself. At this point, the victim will have no other choice than to seek validation from the narcissist about anything they want to do.

6. Isolation from other people

Narcissists take their cruelty further, doing anything they can to push their victim's friends and kin away. Victims of this form of abuse will also intentionally isolate themselves because they feel ashamed of their situation, or because they're afraid no one will understand them, and thus they feel it's best to withdraw and be alone.

Understanding the Tactics of a Narcissist

Neuharth (2017) suggests a number of tactics narcissists employ to victimize the people in their circle. Let's have a look at his list:

1. **Emotional appeals:** This happens when a narcissist plays on the victim's emotions using logic and

reasoning in order to conceal their own false claims and, eventually, control their victim.

2. **Peer groups:** Narcissists join groups where their self-image and ideas are propagated. Within such groups, they feel important and gain a sense of satisfaction because they're with people who support what they do. In turn, they use this to victimize their partner or people around them by mounting pressure on them to join the bandwagon, or make them feel guilty that they're missing out on something good if they don't.

3. **For or against:** Narcissists usually narrow all options to just two: "You're either with me or against me."

4. **Always right:** Narcissists hate to be wrong. If someone tries to prove them wrong, they constantly try to thwart that effort. Even when you spot their errors and successfully point them out, they either dismiss it or change the subject entirely.

5. **False flattery:** Narcissists are as devious and subtle with their compliments as with their critiques. They give insincere compliments because they want something in return.

6. **Labeling:** Narcissists feel most powerful when they're able to attach humiliating labels to their victims.

7. **Empty promises:** Narcissists can easily throw around grandiose promises, but they never have any intention of fulfilling them.

8. **Gaslighting:** Narcissists get at their victims by quoting a part of whatever their victims have said, twisting it, and using it against them. When they do this, they make their victim launch into defensive mode to defend themselves. And when the victim fails at self-defense, which the abuser will ensure happens, they'll begin to doubt themselves. They may even arrive at the point of thinking they've got a dysfunctional mind that can't be trusted to retain information.

9. **Ridicule:** Narcissists don't take other people seriously. They dole out sarcastic comments to ridicule the acts or speech of their victim.

10. **Dehumanization:** Narcissists have a superiority complex. They treat every other person as inferior and they make it obvious, such that people around them feel small and not good enough.

A few other tactics narcissists use are:

- Lying
- Oscillating between cruelty and charm
- Discouragement

- Diminishing others' accomplishments

- Criticism

- Dismissing people

- Stalking

- Intruding

- Emotional blackmail

- Guilt tripping

- Objectifying

- Threats

- Blaming

- Shaming

- Feigning innocence

- Brainwashing

Recovery and Healing from Narcissism

I've met with victims of narcissism who have been so damaged psychologically that they've accepted and adapted to the maltreatment they receive from their narcissistic partner. Sometimes they even feel they deserve what they're getting.

In fact, some become so delusional that they find a way to numb their pain and suffering because they think it's a normal way of life. Others feel their partner truly does love them, and that's why he/she treats them the way they do.

People with such perspectives are difficult to help. Until they're ready to step out of their delusional state, they'll not be free.

It's only those who desire help that'll get it. If you desire to be free and healed and to recover from the psychological abuse you're suffering at the hands of your abuser, here are things I'd suggest you do:

Stage 1: Admit the Truth

- **Admit you're in an abusive relationship:** Some victims of narcissistic relationships don't believe their partner is treating them badly. They believe they deserve what they're getting because their abuser makes it seem so. But until you admit you're being abused, you'll never believe you need help.

  David Tzall, a licensed psychologist in New York, notes (as cited by Cox, 2022) that the first step to healing from a narcissistic relationship is to acknowledge that abuse has occurred and has had a serious impact on your life. Tzall states that admitting this will help you to make sense of your experiences and emotions.

  To get to this point, you'll need to know the signs and symptoms of a narcissistic relationship (I've already written about this in previous sections of this book). This will help you to diagnose your situation and better assess what you're going through.

Educating yourself about this issue is vital to getting to the point of admitting the truth.

- **Admit you're not the problem:** One of the strategies of narcissists is to manipulate the mind of their victim to believe that they're problematic. A narcissist will always point out your errors and weaknesses and make you believe that you deserve to be treated the way you're being treated.

  That's far from the truth. If they're truly helping you to be better, why is it that you've lost your sense of self-worth? How is it that you no longer believe in yourself? Why do you think less of yourself if they've been helping you to be better all this time?

  You're not the problem—they are! It's true you're not perfect, but no one is! Not even your abuser. Therefore, anyone who's using your weakness against you so that they can manipulate you emotionally, and then turn it all on you as if you're the problem, is narcissistic.

- **Admit you need help:** Being in an abusive relationship drains you of a lot of the strength you could have used to ward off your abuser or even get out of the relationship. This is why you need help, and you need to admit it.

  You'll get so little from this book if you don't admit you need help. This book was put together to help you out of that abusive relationship. Your acknowledgment of this will prepare you and open your mind to accept my counsel.

Stage 2: Act Now

- ### Go for the life preserver

  When someone is sinking, a life preserver helps them to stay afloat. Being in a narcissistic relationship is like falling off a ship into a sea of stormy waters. The inability to swim (or navigate the abusive relationship) will naturally put you in danger of drowning. There's no school or institution that prepares you for what to expect in such a relationship. But when it happens, a life preserver will come in handy.

  Your life preserver in this context could be your body. According to the National Alliance on Mental Illness (NAMI), you can heal your mind through your body. Tzall (as cited by Cox, 2022) explains that trauma is stored in the body and mind, but you can release it by engaging in a form of exercise that helps you release the grief, rage, and hurt. Running, kickboxing, and dance cardio are examples of exercises NAMI recommends.

  NAMI also suggests that listening to empowering music or positive affirmations can reinforce the effect of the exercise and help you control your emotions when the negativity you're trying to release starts to get hold of your mind.

A life preserver could also come in the form of engaging in a creative exercise. In 2018, the National Center for Biotechnology Information (NCBI) carried out a study where they asked a group of participants to create artwork based on the theme of nature, religion, and colors. This exercise was carried out in about eight 75-minute sessions. As the participants continued this exercise, they expressed their trauma through their art, but over time the rate at which they did so began to decline; instead, they began to create something more positive.

You can release trauma and its negative effects on you through artistic hobbies like writing, painting, drawing, and playing and/or writing music. You can also share this with the world as proof that healing and recovery from abusive relationships is possible.

Another life preserver could be joining a support group. The good thing about a support group is that you don't have to be ashamed of your experiences because you know you're with people who've had similar journeys. In such a group, you can get the right encouragement and the inner strength you need to confront your psychological issues.

- **Rebuild the hedge**

  Did you remember that one of the things narcissists do is to defy your boundaries and break past your "hedge" into your personal space? They ensure your boundaries are so porous that they can freely intrude any time they want to.

  Continuing on this track of recovery, you can begin to rebuild those boundaries. You could start with securing your personal time so that your abuser cannot intrude or question what you're doing. It could also be something as simple as putting a lock password on your phone.

  You shouldn't be emotional about doing this. Don't worry about what your abuser will think. Just focus your energy on rebuilding the hedge. With that, you can decide who or what goes in or out of your space. Even when your narcissistic partner returns and tries to wriggle back into your space, the boundary will hedge them out, putting *you* in charge of your life once again.

  An important boundary to set is on the definition of who you are. Up till now, you've probably been taking in just about everything your abuser says about you. You must draw a line on that. Take away that right from them. Their comments about who you are shouldn't sway you anymore.

This implies that during this recovery process, you must begin to rediscover your true image. Whatever you discover about yourself is the truth, not what someone who has been taking advantage of you says.

You'll also have to draw the line on the extent to which your abuser can influence your choices. One form of proof that you're no longer under their control is that you can make decisions independent of your abuser. These choices include how you spend your money, where and whom you visit, what and when you eat, and what you wear on your body.

Note: The easiest way to give a narcissist control over your life is to tell them personal things about yourself. They'll gladly take the information and use it to manipulate and hurt you. It's vital that you draw a line on how much of your information you divulge to them, if you need to at all.

- **Plan to set sail again**

  While you're building the hedge, you should also make plans to set sail again. That is, make plans to get your life back on track. While you're in that toxic relationship, you were denied a lot of good things. You sacrificed dreams, purpose, aspirations, wishes, and goals on the altar of narcissism. But the good news is you can set sail again.

Your experience as a victim of a narcissistic relationship might not be so extreme that you lost your job, but a narcissist can still deprive you of some activities that give you pleasure. Think, for example, of the places you wanted to travel but your abuser refused to let you. It's time to make plans for that journey now.

Your life shouldn't be stuck because of someone else. Get your life on track again and do those things you've always loved to do. If you lost a job during the relationship, apply for another, or start your own venture if you'd like. Be enthusiastic to set sail again. You're now the captain of the ship of your life; you can steer the course to whichever direction you desire. Having quieted that external voice that usually dictates the coordinates of your life and got you stuck in the first place, you are now free to set your life in motion again.

Take that professional class. Oh, is it a music lesson or a cooking class you're interested in? Go for it!

You must go for the things you've always imagined doing. There's no better time than now to do them. Stop settling for pseudo-happiness hemmed with tons of regret and self-pity. Your happiness is now your responsibility.

Stage 3: Build Appreciation

- **Forgive yourself**

  In this third stage, the first thing you'll need to do is to forgive yourself. Don't think of it as a one-time thing, either, where you can just say, "Okay, I forgive myself for defending my abuser." That's not enough! Or you might be inclined to say, "I forgive myself. Now what…?"

  Forgiveness doesn't work that way. It's not something you just say casually without being sincere about it.

  This is how forgiveness works on you psychologically: you'll know you've forgiven yourself if you can remember an event that used to make you feel angry and bitter towards yourself, but it no longer does. Generally, the effect of unforgiveness is anger, but when you stop feeling negatively about yourself every time you remember your past mistakes, you're beginning to forgive yourself.

  To forgive yourself is to let go of past hurts.

  Stop holding things against yourself. It can halt this recovery process. You're not stupid to have gone into that relationship in the first place. You went into it because you were in love. And it's not wrong to love. You just didn't see the signs because they were subtly concealed.

However, forgive yourself for choosing to love. Forgive yourself for not seeing the signs. Forgive yourself for defending the abuser. Don't ever blame yourself for those things. You didn't choose a narcissist. It's love you chose, and you can't blame yourself for choosing to love.

If you think you should have known better because you're smart and intelligent, then I need to remind you that you're not a superhuman, and you have emotions too. Anyone, regardless of intelligence, status, or background, could be a victim.

Stop blaming yourself for how the relationship turned out. Accept that you're human and you're prone to mistakes. Admit and embrace your vulnerability, and never feel bad for whatever happens to your abuser.

Repeat this over and over again till your mind is able to let go of the past completely.

- **Anticipate grief**

    If you think that now that you're beginning to get a hold on your life again, you won't have moments of grieving, you're mistaken. Coming out of a traumatic experience causes grief occasionally. You might find yourself longing for your abuser. You might feel sorry for them or consider giving them another chance. There are times you might even feel you miss them because of the days they lavished you with love. You might feel like you shouldn't have left them in the first place. You might blame yourself for not giving them enough chances to get better.

Don't worry, all of these are normal psychological reactions to the grief you're going through. Your mind is taking time to adjust and heal, so you shouldn't expect that all those experiences will be wiped away in a single moment.

Another form of grief you could feel is shame. During your recovery process, there'll be times you reflect on your past experiences and how you got into that situation and feel ashamed of yourself. You could be ashamed that you stooped so low as to accept such maltreatment despite your intellectual, financial, or family status. It could arouse anger and bitterness against yourself.

You could also feel ashamed for ending a romantic relationship you've broadcasted to others in your life so much.

Those feelings are legitimate as well. It's all part of the recovery process. It's just like how medicine that can heal an illness may leave a bitter taste in your mouth. It doesn't negate the fact that you're recovering.

Therefore, don't let any of those feelings get to you. They're transient. They'll dissipate with time.

You can distract your thoughts when you catch yourself in that puddle of negative feelings. Try going over those exercises I recommended in the first stage of recovery again, especially the one that has to do with expressing your emotions through exercise and creative arts. Do this for as long as you need to in order to distract your mind from thoughts of the past.

Get your gaze back on your recovery process!

- **Find *you***

  One of the dangers of being in a narcissistic relationship is that you lose your sense of identity. Your passion, values, and beliefs usually get lost in such a relationship. It's only through the recovery process that you can rediscover yourself. Therefore, during this recovery process, focus your attention on self-rediscovery. You won't be able to find happiness and fulfillment if you're unable to find *you*.

  Rediscover your passion.

  Rediscover your values.

  Rediscover your beliefs.

  Rediscover YOU!

  There's something unique about you. Find it again.

Your voice was silenced in that toxic relationship. You can find it again. Your voice deserves to be expressed. It's been muffled for so long.

This is possible if you begin to practice what I'll recommend next.

- **Cultivate self-love**

Happiness and peace with yourself thrive in the environment of love. In place of the rage and bitterness you used to feel during the traumatic experience, cultivate love. Love emits positive energy against the toxicity of rage and bitterness.

Love yourself without restriction. You have permission to do so. There are many ways you can do this:

- Accept your personality.
- Acknowledge your imperfections and allow yourself to grow during the recovery process.
- Be kind to yourself when you err.
- Learn to choose yourself over and over again as the first person who deserves your attention.
- Prioritize your wellbeing.
- Treat your body with respect by eating good food, resting enough, and exercising properly.
- Always be thankful you survived the traumatic experience.

- Affirm to yourself how unique you are.

- Be patient with yourself during the recovery process.

- Allow yourself to grow at your own pace without comparison to others.

- Be committed to your recovery.

- Don't indulge in self-pity.

- Invest in your growth and mental development.

- Be determined and disciplined to become better daily.

Also, engage in activities that promote your self-esteem, self-worth, and happiness, and that give you a sense of purpose. Be intentional about this.

It's important to note that this process will take time to crystalize into tangible results. You must be persistent and insist on seeing the process through. You deserve to be loved and cared for.

- **Forgive your abuser**

Holding on to the grief of the past is like tying a rock to your neck. Once you dive into the river, you'll drown. No one wants that for themselves. Unforgiveness gives your abuser the power to control your emotions. Whenever you remember all you went through at their hands, you'll certainly feel embittered, but this will only arouse negative energy in you, even though they're no longer with you. Don't give them that much power again.

Forgive them. Let go. It's not possible to forget the experience totally, but you can choose how you respond to it whenever you remember it. Instead of feeling bitterness and rage towards your abuser, be compassionate towards them. They're suffering, but they don't know it. Speak to yourself as if you were talking to them: "Though I feel awful about everything you did to me, I won't allow you to hurt me any further. I choose to let go. I forgive you. I want peace. I want happiness. If I don't forgive you, I'll still have the gall of bitterness in my heart. So for my sake, I forgive you."

You might not choose to say those exact words—feel free to use your own—but repeat it over and over again every time you remember your abuser.

- **Craft your experience into a tool**

  Having experienced what it means to be a victim of a narcissistic relationship and, now, an independent soul, take time to reflect on the lessons you learned from those experiences. You can use those lessons to help so many other people out of that situation. For example, Melody Beattie, author of *Codependent No More: How to Stop Controlling Others and Start Caring for Yourself,* decided to write the book after having been codependent herself. Now, her books are helping lots of people in similar situations beyond what she could ever have imagined.

You might not become a writer. But even if it's a small community you're going to raise around you, go ahead and do just that. The most important thing is that you're helping other people get out of darkness and into light.

Become the lifesaver that throws life preservers to drowning souls when they cry out for help.

- **Don't rush into another relationship**

Dear reader, enjoy your independence! Don't be in a rush to get into another relationship when you're yet to fully recover from the hurts of the previous one.

Allow yourself to heal. Then allow yourself to find yourself and live to the fullest. Don't be under any pressure to jump into a new relationship. Just enjoy your independence. Take time to develop your relationships with people. You don't have any obligation to go beyond the surface level in your relationships with anyone just yet, and that includes your close relatives, colleagues, or neighbors. Don't doubt your ability to love someone again, but give it time.

Workbook Three
Exercise One

Write down three instances when someone you care about made you feel devalued or worthless.

_____

_____

_____

Would you call this person from the answer above a narcissist?

_____

_____

_____

Which of the narcissistic tactics do you feel you've suffered from the most?

(Examples: gaslighting, victim playing, projection, etc.)

_____

_____

_____

How long have you been dealing with this narcissist?

_____

_____

_____

Do you feel like you're too weak to break free from them?

_____

_____

_____

If yes, why do you think you're weak?

_____

_____

_____

If not, what attributes or advantages do you have right now that put you a step ahead of this narcissist? Write down five of these.

_____

_____

_____

What will you do if the narcissist fights back?

_____

_____

_____

Based on the information in this chapter, what do you think is the next best thing for you to do now?

_____

_____

_____

Do you have support systems to help you as you break away from the narcissistic relationship? Write down these people's names and why you've chosen them.

(E.g., "Aunt Mary because she's kind and has been there for me in the past.")

_____

_____

_____

Chapter Three Takeaway

Codependency and narcissism are two negative behavioral patterns that ruin relationships. They're direct opposites that attract like magnets. If you're codependent, chances are that a narcissist is in your life. However, regardless of the impact of the damage, there's hope for redemption. Healing and recovery are possible, as this chapter has proven.

PART TWO

Solutions That Work

My goal as an author is to encourage all my readers to become the best version of themselves, they can. This is in spite of anything they might have been through at any phase of their life. And speaking of things people go through, toxic relationships are one of the most common situations people get into, unplanned, that almost always reduce their chances of becoming the best they could be in life.

So, I've decided to tell you everything you need to know about toxic relationships in this part of the book. I'll also talk about a specific behavioral pattern I believe to be toxic and that could inhibit your chances of living your best life. And, as with the previous part, I'll guide you through the nitty-gritty details of eradicating toxic relationships and behavior from your life.

This is where you get to see the power you have to take charge of your life and destiny through assertiveness. Don't skip any chapter in this part. Each chapter connects to the rest, and they could help to illuminate your life. Now, let's dive in!

CHAPTER FOUR

Understanding Toxicity in Relationships

"The fear of man brings a snare, But whoever trusts in the Lord shall be safe."

—**Proverbs 29:25 (NKJV)**

"Sometimes trying to fix them, breaks YOU."

—**Steve Maraboli**

"Hey, you can't have that!"
"But I'm craving it."
"Well, you still can't have it. The doctor said it's not good for you!"

That was my mom trying to stop my younger self from eating a tasty slice of pizza covered in ketchup, just the way I liked it. I tried to protest, but she insisted, and she won. The dermatologist had told her to take away some things from my regular intake if she really wanted my face to be free from acne. Pizza was one of those foods. She didn't hate me, but I felt like she did because she made me eat more veggies. I didn't know any better then, but now I see it all. I know why she had to ignore my incessant whining to ensure acne didn't take away my self-esteem. I sneaked a few pieces behind her back sometimes; she caught me most times. She showed no sympathy; rather, she ensured I got used to the new eating routine. I share this now because it all paid off, not just for acne, but for my overall health.

You'll need to have my mom's attitude if you want to get rid of toxic relationships in your life. You need to just… lose them. Delete them. Remove them from your life. Rip them off your skin. Need I say more? What else is there to do anyway? Toxic relationships involving things like codependency and narcissism, in most cases, stick on you for a long time, like acne, till you lose your beautiful self. But the good thing is that you can get rid of them if you just have the right attitude and persistence.

A Background Thought

Does anyone set out to have a toxic relationship? I doubt anyone would. Any sane human being desires to have a healthy relationship. But what many people don't know is that even a healthy relationship requires lots of effort to be healthy. And it's not just a one-sided effort. Both parties must be committed to the health of the relationship.

Here's why:

None of us grew up as perfect people. We all have flaws in our behavior, mannerisms, upbringing, and other things that have contributed to our character and personality. Many of us are warped in some ways. But within each of us is also a wealth of goodness. So, we're neither totally perfect nor totally warped.

From day to day, we meet people—from our home to the street, and at school or our place of worship or workplace. We meet people everywhere. Things go sour if our imperfection rules the day. But we'll be the happiest people if we keep our imperfections at bay.

What makes a relationship healthy in spite of our imperfections? It's the commitment of the parties involved to learning how to accommodate and adapt to the other's imperfections. Not only that, but we also must learn to accommodate the other person's personality, ideals, and perspectives, and adapt to their moods. This effort must be mutual to make the relationship healthy.

The difficulty experienced in relationships (which could mutate into toxicity) is dependent on the people in the relationship. A relationship itself is neutral; it's the parties in the relationship that determine what kind of relationship it will be. Difficult partners will have a difficult relationship. Difficult children will have a difficult relationship with their parents, and vice versa. If you apply that to any context of relationships, the same will hold true.

The more difficult the relationship, or the people in the relationship, the more work will be required. Anyone who values their relationship will put in that work.

Toxicity in relationships sets in when the parties involved don't want to accept their imperfections, and they're not ready to put in any effort to make the relationship work. Such nonchalance has the potential to harm one or both people.

But how do you know if your relationship is toxic? That's what I'm about to show you.

What Are Toxic Relationships? How Do They Encourage Codependency?

When a professional in the medical field says something is "toxic," it means that thing is not good for you. It's usually associated with things we eat or take into our body. Generally, when we think of "toxic," something poisonous comes to mind. Regardless of the way you define it, "toxic" doesn't sound great. It never comes off like a word that connotes something delicious. So, let's just hit it straight on the head: anything labeled toxic is poisonous! It's bad.

A relationship can be toxic, too. What does that mean? Yeah, you guessed right: it's a bad relationship! It's a relationship that's poisonous. It's not good for the wellbeing of anyone, and that includes you.

Let's take that a little further. A toxic relationship creates a sense of discomfort, like any poisonous substance will do. Scott (2022) describes a toxic relationship as any relationship where someone feels unsupported, misunderstood, humiliated, or assaulted. She adds that some toxic relationships involve threats to one or both people's emotional, psychological, or even physical wellbeing.

Cory (2022) similarly describes a toxic relationship as a relationship made up of behavioral patterns that damage the other partner emotionally and, more often than not, physically too.

Basically, a relationship that makes you feel worse instead of adding real value to you will evolve into a toxic relationship (Scott, 2022). You'll be amazed to discover that this kind of thing happens in different contexts as well—on the playground, in an elitist boardroom, and even in the bedroom.

A relationship can also be toxic when one of the parties in the relationship takes all the responsibility for keeping the peace while the other person keeps doing things to tear it apart. Unfair, right? It's a lot of hassle to be the only one putting in all the effort. Sacrificing your time, resources, personal space, vision, goals, and more for a one-sided relationship is beyond tedious.

Such effort is commendable, but it's not the healthiest thing to do. It could lead to codependency, especially when you're not being appreciated for your efforts. Let's look at a case study.

Marlyss was a typical example of a person who put so much into her relationship, but it didn't turn out well. She was an attractive woman and a good wife, and she spent most of her time living up to that title. She was always busy taking care of her five children and her husband, who was a recovering alcoholic. She made it her priority to prove that she was a good wife and mother, devoting her life to making her family happy. Unfortunately, she didn't succeed. She grew frustrated over how difficult it was to carry out her role. Coupled with that, she felt unappreciated for her efforts. Instead of appreciating her, her family complained to her. She got even angrier.

But she didn't stop trying. She kept putting a lot of effort into keeping her relationship with her husband healthy, but this drained her and made her lose the good years of her life. She resented this so much, but she felt guilty whenever she wasn't making any effort to live up to that standard of being a good wife and mother.

Marlyss' relationship turned toxic. That wasn't her intention. She planned to make her family happy, but she was doing it alone and she ended up becoming codependent, bearing the full weight of keeping her family afloat while slowly being crushed under that weight.

Another interesting example is Randell. He grew up with an alcoholic father and three alcoholic brothers. He wasn't enjoying his relationship with them, so, as a smart and sensitive young man, he spent a large chunk of his free time obsessing over helping his alcoholic relatives. He tried to clean up the messes they created with the aim of fostering a serene environment where they all could enjoy a healthy relationship. But it didn't work as expected.

Nonetheless, he felt obligated to them. Sometimes he got upset because the people around him behaved in such absurd ways, and he wondered why. He felt sorry for them, and felt he needed to get involved in their problems. To him, that was kindness, love, and genuine concern. But at what expense? He rarely had fun; instead, he spent all his time bearing the burden of other people's issues.

Randell was also codependent; he was committed to "fixing" his relatives or making them better in order to have a healthy relationship with them—but that, too, is toxic. He alone was laden with a yoke meant for two people, each pulling their own weight in the relationship.

When only one person is doing the work—that's a toxic relationship.

Signs You're in a Toxic Relationship

Toxic Relationship Main Signs

Unwillingness to compromise

No respect for boundaries

Breached communication

Excessive arguments

Full of name calling

Competitive

One-sided

Some poisonous substances don't look dangerous. They could be packaged in a shiny cover, and you only discover they're unhealthy after you've consumed them. Similarly, the toxicity of a relationship is not always obvious from the outset. Even though the signs of a toxic relationship are not the same in every context, there are some common ones, and we'll go over those. But ultimately, there's only one person who can tell how bad or good your relationship is: you.

In a general sense, any relationship that constantly threatens your wellbeing through words, actions, or inaction is likely a toxic relationship. It's also important to note that any relationship that involves physical or verbal abuse is absolutely toxic.

These are other signs that indicate a relationship is toxic. These include:

1. Breached communication

Communication is the foundation of any relationship. Relationships grow when the lines of communication, verbal or nonverbal, are intact. The moment that line is broken, bad things are bound to ensue.

Lack of communication causes friction in the relationship. When you stop talking, you'll start stepping on each other's toes. You'll misunderstand each other's actions and inaction. You'll fight over every little thing because you don't have sufficient information to understand the other person; you only act on assumptions. Assumptions can be dangerous in any relationship, and they're also a sign that the relationship is turning sour.

2. Defensiveness

Some psychologists believe that arguing in a relationship isn't all that bad if handled correctly. It's believed that a healthy argument will take the relationship to a deeper level of understanding and intimacy. According to Jane Greer (as cited by Del Russo, 2017), arguments are healthy when you have a specific reason for the fight and a specific problem you're trying to solve. During this kind of argument, there's no devaluing of each other or calling of names. Both parties are able to listen to each other.

But an argument becomes toxic when you become defensive and critical of each other, or you blame one another. Instead of finding compromise, you argue unendingly till you no longer have the strength to continue, and the matter remains unresolved. Later, when something as trivial as who should empty the trash comes up, the bigger, unresolved issue will rear its ugly head to fuel your reaction in this smaller issue.

3. Competition instead of complementing

Have you seen partners who are always competing against each other? I've seen a few. The end result usually isn't good. Each person in the relationship ought to complement the efforts of the others to get better results. The moment we start competing against our partner, we'll be pulling each other down rather than building each other up in order to ensure we're the only one sitting at the pinnacle of success. Competitiveness in any relationship is a sign that the relationship is toxic.

4. Resentment

It's dangerous when partners hold grudges against each other. It's a sure route to distrust and distance. If you tend to nurse grievances quietly for whatever reason, and you can't trust your partner to listen to your concerns, you're quietly breeding a toxic relationship.

5. Glossing over issues

If you never talk about important matters like finances, division of chores, interests, future goals, and values, your relationship could end up being toxic. These topics are important to people and are part of our everyday lives. When the person you're in a relationship with doesn't seem to show interest in or care about your opinions on these things, it could lead to strain in the relationship, and eventually unending fights.

The Dynamics of a Toxic Romantic Relationship

A romantic relationship occurs, typically, between two people who have an intimate connection based on attachment, mutual understanding, interdependence, and a sense of fulfillment. A simpler way of putting this is that when two people are in love with each other and committed to each other, their relationship includes making each other happy.

Love is a beautiful thing. There is no bitterness, envy, hatred, or fear in love. When any of those negative behavioral traits begin to manifest in a romantic relationship, the relationship will become toxic.

A toxic romantic relationship is characterized by the following behavioral patterns:

- Jealousy
- Isolation
- Lack of respect
- Possessiveness
- Emotional and/or physical abuse
- Dominance
- Gaslighting
- Strain in communication
- Manipulation
- Desperation
- Selfishness
- Rejection

This list is not exhaustive, but it'll guide you to identify the negative patterns in your own relationship.

Workbook Four
Exercise One: For Partners

Understanding your relationship is key. Can you confidently say your relationship is healthy and not toxic? The questions below will help you decipher the nature of your relationship. Be honest with yourself when answering the questions.

1. How often do you talk to your partner?

_____

_____

2. Have you ever felt disrespected during an argument with your partner?

_____

_____

3. If yes, give one example.

_____

_____

4. Is your partner a rival to you?

_____

_____

5. Does your partner still love you like before?

_____

6. Can you independently make decisions for your partner?

_____

_____

7. Does your partner degrade your emotions?

_____

_____

8. When did you last engage in an activity with your partner?

_____

_____

9. Do you engage in name-calling in your relationship?

_____

_____

10. How often do you discuss critical issues with your partner?

_____

_____

11. Based on your above answers, would you say your relationship is toxic?

_____

_____

Exercise Two: Toxic Family Cycles

Is your family of origin toxic?

_____

_____

If your answer to the previous question was yes, why?

_____

_____

Do you think you'll ever be able to draw boundaries with them?

_____

_____

How do you propose to do that?

_____

_____

Which family member(s) is/are particularly toxic, in your opinion? Add one reason why you mentioned this person/these people.

(E.g., "James, because he's the golden child and always wants everything to go his way.")

_____

_____

Do you still want to have a relationship with your family of origin?

_____

_____

How do you hope to set boundaries from this point on for these particularly annoying folks?

(E.g., "Inform James he's no longer allowed to come to my house unannounced.")

_____

_____

Chapter Four Takeaway

Personally, I don't believe that there are certain people for whom you *can't* set boundaries. There's always a way, and that's what I communicated in this chapter. If you're dealing with a toxic relationship and you're ready to break free, the ball is in your court. You'll no longer be responsible for anyone else's mess. You're becoming responsible for yourself, and as a person who is recovering from codependency in leaps and bounds, this chapter is your cue to say no with love.

CHAPTER FIVE

Putting an End to People Pleasing

"For do I now persuade men, or God? Or do I seek to please men? For if I still pleased men, I would not be a bondservant of Christ."

—Galatians 1:10 (NKJV)

"I finally know the difference between pleasing and loving, obeying and respecting. It has taken me so many years to be okay with being different, and with being this alive, this intense."

— Eve Ensler

Maybe you have a general idea of what people pleasing is, but let's go a little deeper into exactly what that means. Professor Alena Papayanis shares her personal story of people pleasing in a Huffington Post article; while she was in college, she dated a "sweet" guy who never matched the effort she put into their relationship. The guy's dad cautioned her not to do everything for him or try to be *too* nice to him, but she didn't understand this advice.

She tried to balance the deficit in their relationship by being overly nice. She tried hard for both of them. By giving herself to the relationship fully, she thought she'd become indispensable and it would be impossible for the guy to reject her. She felt her niceness would shield her from ever being abandoned. Turns out, that was wrong.

Nevertheless, Papayanis carried this perception long into adulthood until she realized that she was not just being nice— she was being a people pleaser, and this was dangerous because it kept her boxed in, unseen, and unfulfilled for decades.

Before you start thinking you'll stop being nice to people, you should read this out loud to yourself: It's not just being nice that makes you a people pleaser; it's being *overly* nice, to the point that **you** get lost in the niceness. That's a pretty accurate description of people pleasing.

People Pleasing Is Not Selflessness

To illustrate this point, let's take a look at an example from the Bible. Martha, the sister of Lazarus and Mary of Bethany, thought she was doing the best thing possible by running around, trying to take care of every guest that came into their house uninvited. While everyone else, including her sister, was sitting down, listening to the edifying words of a certain Jewish Rabbi (Jesus) that could transform their lives, Martha was completely wrapped up in trying to please this honored guest.

At the point when the weight of the cooking was crushing her, she complained. She wanted Jesus to take her side and ask Mary to assist her in the kitchen. Martha's sense of hospitality wasn't getting the kind of notice she'd hoped, and she wasn't getting noticed either. So she decided to take it out on her sister, insinuating that Mary was lazy and not as hospitable as she ought to be. If the Rabbi didn't see through this, no one would have thought that her sense of hospitality was turning to hostility. But the Rabbi named it as it was. He told her that her effort at trying to impress Him wasn't necessary. In His judgment, it would have been better if she was seated with everyone else to listen.

Martha might have felt disappointed, but it was the truth. You know how some of us sometimes try to do certain things for someone we honor, love, or have a crush on even when it's not convenient (or it feels like it's killing us)? We might try to convince ourselves that it's an act of selflessness, but at the core of that sentiment, you know it's not. There are other things that make you do what you do.

Let's shine some more light on that behavioral pattern.

People pleasing has a very similar description to concepts such as selflessness, generosity, and kindness. On the surface they look alike; however, a deeper look shows that they're not the same. People pleasing doesn't look good on its practitioners. They go all the way for other people while concealing their pain, smiling like nothing's wrong. So, people get accustomed to seeing them happy all the time and never complaining about anything whatsoever—until the people pleaser can't take it anymore.

In sharing her experience as a recovering people pleaser, Alena Papayanis made it clear that it's misconstruing to associate people-pleasing with being genuinely selfless just because people pleasers show extreme kindness and are sincerely compassionate. Yes they do. That's not all there is to those superficial acts. True kindness doesn't make you betray yourself, and the weight of your kind act shouldn't crush you to the point that you explode in anger, bitterness, and resentment.

During Papayanis's years as a people pleaser, while she was selflessly doing things for other people, her own needs became insignificant. How she felt didn't matter. She was the last person to care about how she felt about anything and was more interested in how everyone else felt. This meant that she wasn't even paying attention to herself. Her needs weren't a priority.

She later found out that her selflessness wasn't true kindness; it was the result of her personal fears and insecurities. She had thought (wrongly) that if she pleased everyone, they'd love her in return. People pleasers tend to believe that nobody loves anyone just for the sake of loving them—that people have to do things and make sacrifices to get anyone to like or accept them.

Such a perspective is wrong, and it has grievous side effects in our relationships. I'll show you how unhealthy it is before I close this chapter.

Many people hold the same mistaken perspective on people pleasing as Martha and Alena Papayanis. And I don't blame them for it. If you're one of them, don't be hard on yourself. Remember that most of us cultivate certain behavioral patterns from our childhood, and others we pick up from our environment or based on our experiences as adults. You're not at fault. This is your moment of truth. Everyone who has gone through some form of toxicity in their relationship and is healing and recovering has had the same moment. This is yours. Don't miss it!

Think of these individuals as examples of true selflessness: William Pitsenbarger, Scott Davidson, Neerja Bhanot, and Martin Luther King Jr. Something fascinating about these folks is that they sacrificed their lives to save many others. Doesn't that sound like people pleasing? No! Here's why:

- They sacrificed for a just cause.
- They weren't seeking attention for themselves. Other people did that for them.
- They didn't feel crushed under the weight of their actions. They carried on till death. Martin Luther King Jr. thought it a glorious thing to lay down his life.
- They found fulfillment in their actions.

- They didn't need people's validation to keep doing what they did.

- Most of the people they saved weren't people they intended to curry favor from. They just did it to preserve life and posterity.

Unfortunately, the same things cannot be said of people pleasing. Here's what happens in people pleasing:

- You're focused on what people think about you.

- You fear criticism, so you try everything you can to get in people's good book, even if it means doing something foolish.

- You're a yes-person. You don't have the courage to say no because you don't want to offend anyone.

- Sometimes you remain passive in making decisions because you don't want to take sides. You don't want to offend anyone on either side.

- You don't have your own defined emotions. You feel how other people feel.

- You're indecisive until the person you're trying to please makes a decision.

- You do everything you can to fit into the pack. You just want to feel accepted.

- Unlike with selflessness, you don't feel fulfillment from what you do. You feel used and drained.

- Anyone can invade your personal space. No boundaries.

- You accept just about everything. You go to any length necessary to please others, not because it feels right, but because you feel satisfied when someone says, "Oh, you're so sweet."

- Your sense of self-worth and self-esteem come from what people think about you.

- Your identity is with the mob. The mob defines what and who you are. And that's what you believe about yourself.

- You regret many of the things you do, and when you're alone you may end up crying over them. Sometimes you resent yourself and think you're not good enough.

This list isn't exhaustive, and it's not possible for one person to manifest all these traits all the time. You could recognize yourself in just parts of what is on that list. But the bottom line is that people pleasing isn't good for you. It's toxic, and it makes you depend on other people to do anything worthwhile with your life. Your relevance and essence will always revolve around people as a people pleaser. But here's the thing: people cannot always be trusted to be nice and never take advantage of you.

Effects of Unhealthy People Pleasing

People pleasing has side effects, and they're not pleasant. You might already know that, but maybe you weren't sure if it was people pleasing causing those effects. Here, we'll highlight the negative aspects of people pleasing.

The most devastating damage people pleasing does is not on your body, but your inner being. Here's what gets affected when you take the path of people pleasing:

Loss of Self

While you struggle to fit into everyone's idea of who they think you are, you lose the real you. You lose your identity while trying to please everyone. All that's visible is what the mob has created. This means that you'll have multiple self-images that appear at different times and in different places. If that sounds weird, it's because it is. Losing your sense of self can be very damaging to your mental health.

Neglected Self

As a people pleaser, your spirit, soul, and body will get little or no care. Your physical health could begin to fail in the process. YI might also begin to quietly lose your mind from trying to fit into everyone's idea of you. You're good at taking care of others—you check up on people to ensure they're fine—yet you can barely end a day without feeling aches all over your body from the stress. Perhaps you've not yet realized that you can't truly take care of people if you're unhealthy yourself.

Loss of Ideals

No one can try to please everyone without losing their core principles. To please everyone, you must be ready to compromise, bending your principles to fit theirs. This is a short route to becoming a puppet that can be controlled at will.

Try to do a personal assessment about your core values right now. Ask yourself:

- What do I stand for?
- What do I believe in?
- What am I without my personal values?

If you don't have answers to those questions, it could be because you've allowed people to define your life the way they deem fit. Humans can be bad puppeteers. They love to take advantage of others when given the chance. And in a real sense, you won't do much in life if you spend all your time trying to please people. At best, they'll use you to get to their destination. And you? You'll be left regretful and angry, feeling you've been used and dumped.

Resentment. Anger. Bitterness.

You'll end up resenting the fact that you never have time for yourself. You use up the time you ought to spend caring for yourself on other people, and now you're worn out. There are things you innately care about, things you wish to get done, but you're just too busy prioritizing other people that don't really care about you. This could lead to resentment, and make you bitterly angry with yourself.

But that changes nothing. It only drains you emotionally.

Your anger will skyrocket if the reason you've been trying to please someone ends up being pointless. But you won't be able to channel your anger to other people—you'll still be the victim of your own outburst. Sometimes you might subtly demonstrate hostility (like Martha did) towards your loved ones, like making little jabs, using sarcastic jokes, or throwing shade. When you try to suppress your resentment, it'll work, but only for a short time. If not nipped in the bud, more negative feelings will show.

Another side effect is that people pleasing can increase your stress level to the point where you no longer find pleasure in anything. The enjoyment you used to derive from certain events or activities is likely to decrease. In a real sense, you don't have time to enjoy anything because you have so many commitments to other people. Even when you're not doing anything, you're constantly thinking of the things you have to do next.

Do you know that this can make you lose good friends? If you no longer show up to an activity that you used to enjoy with your friend or partner, you might lose that relationship in the long run. And that can create even more anxiety for you.

Purposelessness

To be purposeful means that you have a definite destination, vision, or goal. But how can you have a definite place you're going to when other people can intercept you and divert you from your path? And because you want to make people happy, you painfully feign a smile and accept.

What if your vision doesn't align with the vision of your boss or the group you belong to? It dies a natural death even before it starts becoming tangible. And your goals? You'll forget them altogether because you're pursuing something else for someone else.

If this continues, you'll never dare to make plans for anything again because it won't matter in the end. Your ability to aspire to lofty and great things will be maimed because even if you do aspire, it'll only remain a figment of your imagination that can never come to fruition. You'll doubt your ability to ever become anything more than what people want you to be.

This is a dangerous place to be. All your potential and talents will lie dormant and untapped in this state.

Loss of Confidence in Self

When people tell you that you're not good enough or you're not suitable for their group, what happens? You probably feel like your whole world is crumbling. If this is the group of people you've been trying to please, then because you respect their comments more than anyone else's, you believe their words to be true. That could begin to impact how you see yourself and what you think about yourself. That's the moment you begin to think you're a massive failure and you can never excel at anything. You doubt yourself.

When people you're trying to please also constantly trash your opinions, you'll lose confidence in your ability to ever say anything meaningful.

Think of the times you tried to voice your opinion. What happened? Were you heard? How did you react? Your courage dies a natural death every time you are ignored. If you do not do something about this, the idea that your opinions are not worth hearing will grow into your subconscious and sentence you to a life of silence and timidity. You'll tell yourself to always accept what everyone else says and never say anything to the contrary.

Stress

People pleasers are naturally everyone's go-to person. They never say no. Everyone loves to have those kinds of people as team members or as their colleagues.

Even if they have their own piles of work to finish up, a people pleaser will still accept requests for help from others. Just the thought of all that work is exhausting. It's a direct invitation to stress, which will eventually lead to a breakdown. When you take on more than you can handle, you'll always be a victim of health issues. That's not difficult to diagnose.

Unfortunately, you're not a superhuman. No one can constantly shoulder their own burdens plus the burdens of other people and remain mentally and physically healthy. Thus, you've been endangering yourself.

How to Create a Balance – Selflessness Can be Balanced

I'm an advocate of selflessness. I hope I've made that obvious to you. But I'm also a realist. I've had enough experience with people to know what they're capable of.

Not everyone sees things the way you see them, so don't assume that while you're transforming from people pleasing to genuine selflessness, things will go smoothly right away. There are people out there who will want to take advantage of your genuineness.

Before you think it's not possible to live harmoniously with people, let me drive this sentiment home to you: selflessness is a virtue that can build nations.

But there's a balance to selflessness, too—one that won't make you be at the beck and call of everyone else, all in the name of trying to be selfless. Now, we don't want you to crawl back into people pleasing. But while I try to create a balance here, your knowledge of the distinction between people pleasing and selflessness will come in really handy. (You might need to go over that distinction again before continuing.)

So, how do you live selflessly without being a people pleaser? Here's how:

Eliminate Feelings of Guilt

You must learn to eliminate any guilt that pops up. Selflessness does not mean you'll say yes to every request. Thus, you shouldn't feel guilty for turning someone down. If it's a task that would not fit well with your schedule or simply something you don't want to do, don't do it. Kindly decline and move on. A people pleaser will feel guilty for declining a request. But that's no longer you! You're coming out of that already.

Don't Judge Yourself Based on One Action

Don't label yourself as cruel or selfish for declining a request. Being selfless or otherwise is largely about your behavioral response in certain circumstances. That doesn't mean that's who you are. You could learn to be a genuinely selfless person, but there are situations that would warrant acting selfishly. That doesn't make you a selfish person; you just made the best decision for yourself as the occasion demanded.

Therefore, you shouldn't tag yourself as being selfish just because of one circumstance. People are free to call you anything they want, but you should resolve in your heart that you're not other people's labels.

Be Prepared to Own Your Decisions

Be bold enough to own your decision to act selflessly (or not) in any given situation. If you choose a behavior, stand by it. That means you'll also have to face the outcome of the decision head on. Even if it doesn't turn out great, you can take solace in the fact that you made an independent choice without being intimidated by how people might think or what they might say about you.

Mix Selflessness with a Bit of Selfishness

MMA fighter and motivational speaker Charlie Brenneman has a good description of this on his blog. Brenneman explains how he had to make an important decision for himself and his marriage, and since he was in a relationship, his decision wasn't about him alone; he had to be considerate of his partner. That sounds like a **selfless** thing to do. But he also had a clear vision for his UFC career, and he made it his priority. This sounds

selfish. But the motive for his pursuit was to be able to inspire other people to attain their greatest self. Now that sounds **selfless**. But to achieve any of that, he had to be in a good state of mind. That's **selfish**.

Oscillating between selflessness and selfishness like this could seem daunting, but it's not so hard to do. Here are some tips:

Admit You Need the Self-Care

Hagar (2023) notes that it's important to learn to fill our own cup first (that is, take care of our needs first), not only for our personal wellbeing but also for the wellbeing of others. Self-care might seem selfish, but we can only give as much goodness to people as we have in ourselves. It's only right to ensure we are mentally and physically healthy in order to have healthy relationships with other people.

Take care of yourself. When you practice self-care, you're responding to your personal needs while at the same time considering the impact of your own good health on the people around you.

Dig Deep Enough to Give More

Naturopathic doctor Sherwood (2021) reiterates the golden rule to love others as much as you love yourself. In his view, we are stewards of our lives, and our key responsibility is to cater to our own needs.

He uses the analogy of digging a well to explain the balance between selfishness and selflessness. To get a sufficient amount of good water from a well, you have to dig deep. In the same way, putting enough work into your spiritual, emotional, and physical wellbeing is not really all that selfish. According to Sherwood, it's actually an extreme act of selfishness to fail to take care of yourself, as you'll become a liability to the people around you. Therefore, you must make the right choices regarding your lifestyle.

Create a Serene Environment

Pablo (2021) adds his thoughts to this discourse as well, stating that the beautiful balance to be found in living life to the fullest is in learning to look out for yourself and your interests—but also the understanding that the greatest form of fulfillment comes from helping others. You give love, you get love in return. But how can you give what you don't have?

Pablo warns against overdoing self-care to the point of hurting people. He also suggests weighing the need and the circumstance before acting selflessly. For example, it's not right to go bankrupt for a drug addict who's not willing to change. You don't need to defend or support someone who's acting badly and doesn't intend to improve their behavior. You'll only be subjecting yourself to constant ridicule and unfair treatment in your supposed act of selflessness.

It's not smart to give away what you need yourself. Don't become a beggar to feed a beggar. Nothing will change that way.

Both Matter

This is what I consider to be the peak of the middle ground between selfishness and selflessness. Don't prioritize one over the other. Don't make the mistake of focusing on self-care while you lack in generosity to others. You can do both. As you create time for yourself, also schedule time to be with your friends or to do things for people in need. It's not a matter of you versus them. Both matter. This mindset will help you form healthy relationships with others.

You can have healthy relationships without crawling to people as if they hold the key to your self-worth. You can independently care for yourself and still be selflessly generous towards others, but not at your own detriment.

Workbook Five

Exercise One: Are You a People Pleaser?

People pleasers are prone to certain behaviors. This exercise will help to pinpoint some of these characteristics in yourself. Having more yeses than no's in this exercise means you're definitely a people pleaser.

Tick either yes or no.

NUMBER	QUESTIONS	YES	NO
1.	Do you have principles?		
2.	Do you easily change your plans for people?		
3.	Do you seek people's approval?		
4.	Do you complain or nag when you're working?		
5.	Have you ever gotten to a point where you lack enjoyment in everything you do?		
6.	Are you selfish?		
7.	Do you easily judge yourself?		

8.	Do you say "yes" to everyone's requests?		
9.	Do you feel guilty for not giving a positive response to people's requests?		
10.	Do people take you for granted at your workplace?		
11.	Do you feel purposeless?		
12.	Do you get angry when no one notices your effort on a project?		

Exercise Two: Debunking Myths

What myths did you use to believe about people pleasing? Write four.

_____

_____

_____

_____

Based on what you know now, would you say people pleasing is cool? Give reasons for your answer.

_____

_____

_____

_____

Do you still want to remain a people pleaser? Why or why not?

_____

_____

_____

_____

What's your game plan to stop people pleasing?

_____

_____

_____

_____

Chapter Five Takeaway

Selflessness and people pleasing are not the same. You can be selfless without losing your mind. You can be selfless without being a doormat. Yes, I said it. At this point, you really need to come to terms with the fact that you've only got one life, and you can't spend all of it pleasing people. In a healthy relationship, the needs of both parties will be equally prioritized, rather than one person's needs being more important.

We're more than halfway through this book, and by now I really hope you've started to think about your life. People pleasing will hurt you badly. You've got to move on from it.

So far, if you have learned something from the book, please click here to leave a review on Amazon. That will help other people in their personal development.

CHAPTER SIX

The Assertiveness and Boundary Setting Guide

"A soft answer turns away wrath, But a harsh word stirs up anger."

—Proverbs 15:1 (NKJV)

"Assertiveness is asking for what you want, turning others down, and making decisions that are right for you without anger, threats, manipulation, or fear of repercussions."

—Patrick King

Earlier in this book, I mentioned the crucial role of communication in a relationship. Communication involves more than just talking. For you to be taken seriously and as someone who is capable of making independent choices, you must learn to communicate your thoughts assertively. That's how to let people know that you know what you're doing.

Are you just recovering from a toxic relationship? This is an important lesson for you.

Learning to Be Assertive

Speed et al. (as cited by Sutton, 2021) describe assertiveness as "standing up for oneself without significant anxiety, expressing one's feelings comfortably, or exercising one's own rights without denying the rights of others." When you lack assertiveness, you won't be able to do any of those things. This can tilt towards people pleasing and hostility, as well.

Here's a practical example of assertiveness. My uncle asked his daughter to send a message to their realtor about getting an electrician to come and fix something at the house. Here's what my cousin typed:

- "I'd like the electrician to come this morning."
- My uncle told her not to send that message. He said this would be better:
- "Tell the electrician to come this morning."
- Which of the two sounds more assertive?

My uncle's wording sounds authoritative and stern. His approach is a mild form of aggression in a conversation. But being aggressive doesn't make you assertive. At best, it'll send the wrong message to the recipient. On the other hand, my cousin's wording makes it sound like she's pleading, but her message is nevertheless assertive. The request was serious, but she didn't make it sound that way (which could put the other person under unnecessary pressure). She knew what she wanted, she was clear about it, and she stated it concisely.

Assertiveness is an essential communication skill (Mayo Clinic Staff, n.d.). Being assertive during communication allows you to express your thoughts more effectively and makes you sound like you know what you're talking about.

Since assertiveness is a communication skill, it can be learned. Even though you may have lost the confidence to speak up for yourself during a toxic relationship, now that you're going through a period of recovery, you can learn to find your voice again.

Perhaps knowing the benefits of being assertive will motivate you to learn. Being assertive will:

- Boost your self-esteem
- Help you to earn other people's respect
- Help you manage stress by declining requests to take on responsibilities that may wear you out
- Make you more likely to get what you want
- Improve your communication with others
- Let you create honest relationships with people around you
- Help you create healthy boundaries

Now, are you convinced you need to learn this communication skill?

This is how to be assertive during any communication:

Start with "I," Not "You"

During a conversation, when you start sentences with "you," you're unintentionally putting the other person on the spot. Oftentimes the other person will naturally jump into defensive mode. But when you start with "I," the other person will see things from your perspective and listen to what you have to say.

For instance, instead of saying, "You're wrong," start with, "I disagree."

When you want to make a request, you can say, "I would like you to help with…" instead of, "You need to…"

An article from Coursera illustrates this concept well and provides a formula for this kind of conversation. Follow this pattern:

"I feel ____ when ____ because ____. What I need/ want is ____." (Coursera, 2023)

For example, "I feel disrespected when you talk back to me in public. Could you correct me when we're alone together, instead?"

Here's another example: "I was already loaded up with different tasks when you asked me to help you with yours."

Using this formula will help you to express how other people's behavior makes you feel in a respectful way, instead of pointing an accusing finger and putting them on the defensive.

Softly Decline with a Smile

Having been a yes-person for a while, you need to set your boundaries and prioritize your wellbeing. I suggest you learn to say no. Of course, you won't just start saying it with all the audacity with which you've been wanting to say it for so long; internally, you might feel a bit unsure about saying it, but do not let that be reflected in your voice.

The next time a request comes asking you to take on more responsibilities, softly say, "No" with a smile. It could turn out to be the best thing you've done for yourself in a long while.

According to recent research, the stress that comes with overwork could lead to serious health problems such as sleeplessness, depression, diabetes, heart disease, damaged memory, and decreased productivity (Carmichael, 2015). This is to say that accepting every task that comes your way can have serious long-term effects.

Hold Firm to Your Decision

Not everyone easily takes no for an answer. They'll love to push further to get you to change your mind, testing your resolve and looking for a hole in your armor—a weak spot they can use to get through to you.

In that moment, weigh the impact of their request on you. If complying will not do you much good, or will be harmful for you, insist on your initial response. Don't argue with them. Just persist in saying no with a smile on your face. You can add "sorry" when you're declining the second time if you'd like to. You could even give them an alternative option or refer them to someone else. But hold firm to your response.

Body Language Matters

Nonverbal communication has always been important, but it's even more relevant in our post-Covid-19 world (Michail, 2020). It's become a part of our daily existence. The pandemic forced us to learn how to communicate more with gestures, eye contact, and other nonverbal means. According to body language research, 7% of all communication is verbal, whereas the tone of our voice and our body language represent 38% and 55% respectively.

This means that learning to communicate with body language comes with great rewards for assertiveness. You can act confidently, even if you don't feel confident. Here's how:

Sit upright, leaning forward a bit. Make regular eye contact. Keep a neutral or positive facial expression. Don't cross your arms or legs. You can rehearse this in front of a mirror or with a friend before having a conversation you're nervous about to help you master the art.

Learning assertiveness could take a while, but if you persist, it'll pay off in the long term.

Balancing Assertiveness with Compassion

Public speaking coach Sims Wyeth (2015) notes that leadership "is a constant tug between assertiveness and empathy."

While empathy nudges you to show understanding towards what others are thinking and feeling, assertiveness involves expressing yourself confidently (without being aggressive).

Have you met people who couldn't cope with your standard of assertiveness? It's true that you're trying to create a system for yourself that will ensure no one takes advantage of your selflessness and generosity, but you still need to balance that assertiveness with empathy.

Research shows that empathy, compassion, and understanding for others are three things that give us the peace and happiness we desire. As much as we want and need to create boundaries to protect ourselves, we must also balance those boundaries with the skill of empathy. This will help us to express ourselves confidently while maintaining a consideration for the feelings of the other person.

Here's how to do it:

Analyze the Situation

You can choose which behavioral pattern to display depending on the situation. Analyze the situation first, then choose to either be assertive first, then show empathy, or vice versa. Remember that you're dealing with different people in different contexts; you can't expect the circumstances or the personalities involved to always be the same. Analyze first, then decide on how to respond.

Learn to Listen and Pay Attention to Details

To effectively analyze the situation, you must learn to be a good listener with a good eye for detail. Listening is a great empathy skill. You're able to show empathy when you see things from another person's perspective, not by watching their emotional displays (these could be deceptive), but by paying close attention to their speech and intuiting how they might be feeling.

Go Head-First, Then Follow with the Heart

Empathy is a skill that allows us to build great relationships in different contexts. You need a good heart to show empathy. With a compassionate heart, you can be considerate in your decision to be assertive. But before you go all-in with your heart, ensure your head is involved in the interaction. You can see through toxic people's schemes and antics when your head is involved in the exchange. Don't get overly emotional.

Usefulness of Boundaries in Relationships

One of the objectives of this book is to guide individuals on how to end unhealthy relationships and begin to live the life they were designed to live. One of the things that I've suggested to you as an important means to recovering from unhealthy relationships is boundary setting.

This can't be overemphasized. Boundary setting comes with a lot of benefits for someone who wants to live independently of people's selfish interests. Before learning the benefits, let me remind you again what boundary setting looks like.

According to Martin (2016), boundaries are guidelines that inform people how you want to be treated. This includes letting them know what behaviors you will accept and what you won't. This could range from simply letting someone know that they can't keep yelling at you to excusing yourself from a conversation or a group, or blocking someone on your phone.

Now, the benefits of setting boundaries:

- **Helps you set clear expectations:** Having boundaries doesn't make you a mean person. It just helps you to set clear expectations and limits to what you can take and what you can't.

- **Gives a sense of peace and security:** Boundaries protect us from physical and emotional harm. This includes physical violence, unwanted touch, verbal abuse, and manipulation. Boundaries also provide emotional freedom from self-criticism and second-guessing. Personally, when I don't set boundaries, I get stuck in shame and self-doubt. I criticize myself for not asking for respect and allowing others to mistreat me. In contrast, when I set boundaries, I feel empowered and safe.

- **Tones down resentment:** When you don't have boundaries, you're likely to overcommit to things and spend more time on other people's problems than you planned. You'll go overboard to please other people to your own detriment and waste time doing things that don't add any value to you, or even things that go against your values. You might lose your self-worth and identity in the process, as well. You'll do these things with a fake smile on your face while you groan inwardly. When you're alone, you'll probably hate yourself for taking on so much more than you can handle.

When you set boundaries, you're less likely to feel this resentment towards yourself or anyone else because you'll be able to speak up for yourself, and decline whatever will hurt you.

- **Helps you build a better self-image and self-esteem:** Without boundaries, you fit into everything that everyone calls you or says about you. You don't have a defined image of yourself. With boundaries, you can have time to focus on yourself and redefine yourself from your perspective. This will boost your self-confidence and give you a sense of self-worth.

- **Boosts your mental and emotional wellbeing:** With the boundaries you set, you can be free from the mental stress and emotional breakdown that arise from doing everything everyone else wants you to do.

- **Reduces burnout:** When you build boundaries around yourself, you won't take on too many commitments anymore. This way, you'll have ample time to rest and refresh yourself, thus avoiding burnout.

How to Set Boundaries

The need to set boundaries can be different in different contexts and with different people. Some people need to set boundaries with family, others in the workplace, and others in their romantic relationship. Regardless of the context where you need to set boundaries, you have to remember that you're the same person in all contexts. The boundaries you set for one context could be applicable in other situations. Essentially, there are *generic boundaries* and *specific boundaries*.

For instance, if you're the go-to person at work and in your family, people will always want to dump tasks on your lap regardless of the context. When you decide to be assertive in declining people's requests, it'll be reflected in all your relationships. This is a *generic boundary.*

Generally, boundary setting begins with **self-awareness**. You don't like the way you behave in your relationships or you don't like the way people treat you? You can change it. It starts with *you.* It's a form of self-awareness to recognize that you can no longer accept the way things are going in your relationships.

What If My Boundaries Are Disrespected?

The boundaries you set for yourself are meant to improve your wellbeing, but they aren't for you alone; you need the cooperation of other people for the boundaries to be effective.

But what if the other person isn't cooperative? Sounds like another thing to worry about, doesn't it? Don't worry—there's a way around this.

Martin (2016) suggests that you assess your situation first using the following questions.

- Who is disrespecting your boundaries? The type of relationship you have (family member, romantic partner, coworker, etc.) will determine your response.

- Can this person change? Talk with the person to find out whether they're intentionally crossing your boundaries and whether or not they're willing to make a change.

- How long have you been dealing with these boundary violations? If they've been doing this for years, for example, it might be harder for this person to change (though not impossible).

- Is the person being physically violent? At this point, your safety comes first seek a way to get away from them because they're not likely to change anytime soon. Don't hesitate to ask for help from a support group or relative. If you're a minor, you could also reach out to a trusted adult at school, church, or your parent's friends, or a hotline. It's dangerous to assume you can do it alone.

- Are you enforcing your boundaries? Don't assume other people know what they are. Ensure the boundaries you've set are clear to those around you, and more importantly, ensure your response to a violation is always consistent. Don't compromise, regardless of the situation or persons involved. Be consistent in defending your boundaries.

After this analysis, you may decide on any of the following actions to ensure your boundaries are respected (Martin, 2016):

1. **Reiterate them:** In the previous analysis, you identified the person who is violating your boundaries. Perhaps they didn't take you seriously the first time. Restate your boundaries firmly and emphatically, but not

aggressively, over and over again to drive the message home.

2. **Choose your reaction:** Some people intentionally violate your boundaries to get a reaction out of you. You can choose how you respond. Instead of allowing them to anger you, choose to laugh instead or just silently leave the situation. It'll make a huge difference.

3. **Accept what you can't change:** The only person you have control over is you. Don't expect to change people by setting boundaries. If the person who is disrespecting your boundaries refuses to change, you can either re-strategize regarding how to communicate your boundaries to them, or find other ways to keep yourself protected from their negative influence.

Workbook Six
Exercise One: Violated Boundaries

What boundaries have you set in the past? Write down five.

_____

_____

_____

_____

Do you agree that setting boundaries has saved you a lot of trouble? Summarize your view on this.

_____

_____

_____

_____

_____

_____

_____

Who has violated your boundaries in the past? What did you do when those boundaries were violated?

_____

_____

_____

_____

_____

_____

_____

_____

Exercise Two: Setting Boundaries

Write down five people in your life for whom you feel you need to set boundaries.

_____

_____

_____

_____

What barriers do you feel you're likely to face when setting boundaries for these people?

_____

_____

_____

_____

How do you hope to overcome these barriers in order to make your boundary setting a successful venture?

_____

_____

_____

_____

_____

_____

_____

_____

Chapter Six Takeaway

Abusers, narcissists, and other toxic people who are out to prey on the vulnerable will never take kindly to boundaries. They will try to convince you that boundaries are unnecessary. You now know that boundaries are extremely important. Of course, you can have boundaries and still be kind to people.

PART THREE

Complete Healing Is Possible

Back in high school, when I was a senior, it seemed like everyone was in a relationship. It was important to be liked and to like someone. Everybody knew this and strove to be accepted. Everyone. But not my best friend, Zoey.

Happily, for me, the girl I liked, liked me back, and we started dating—but unfortunately, I crossed a line before I realized what was happening. Maybe it was because my tender heart was still too immature to handle matters of love, but anyway, I grew really paranoid and jealous. I imagined my girlfriend cheating on me, and I accused her of doing so, too, until I finally pissed her off and she dumped me.

In the midst of my pain and regret, I sought comfort from Zoey.

Do you think I should call her?

Should I get her flowers?

Do you think buying her an expensive dress would fix this?

I tried to make him tell me what to do. Instead, Zoey only said, "You don't need a relationship right now, man."

The more he said that, the more annoyed I got. My turning point, however, came when he stood up on the park bench we'd been sitting on, spread his arms in the air, and said, "Unlike y'all, I'm free as a bird." Then he lunged forward to jump off the bench, flapping his arms like wings, and gave me a smile.

I saw that contented look of freedom in his eyes, and instantly I knew: *I wanted that.*

Let me ask you: Do you want freedom, too? Are we on the same page here? I sure hope so!

In this final part of the book, I'm going to emphasize something: You can be completely healed. You can *completely* offload that heavy burden and become free. True and total freedom is possible. And we're about to get into the "how" for that.

CHAPTER SEVEN

Independence and Interdependence

"Brethren, if a man is overtaken in any trespass, you who are spiritual restore such a one in a spirit of gentleness, considering yourself lest you also be tempted. Bear one another's burdens, and so fulfill the law of Christ."

—Galatians 6:1, 2 (NKJV)

"In the progress of personality, first comes a declaration of independence, then a recognition of interdependence."

—Henry Van Dyke

Before I walk you through this final part, I want you to read this out loud to yourself:

A HEALTHY RELATIONSHIP IS POSSIBLE. I DESERVE TO HAVE A HEALTHY RELATIONSHIP. I CAN HAVE A HEALTHY RELATIONSHIP.

Repeat that to yourself till you're convinced of what you're saying.

Independence vs. Codependency

If you've been around for a while, you've almost certainly heard of America's Declaration of Independence. In the late 18th century, the North American colonies of Great Britain revolted against British rule to secure one thing: independence. They were tired of being controlled. They didn't want to be told what to do and what not to do by Britain, so they revolted.

Why would anyone want to be independent, and why would they fight with everything they have in order to get it? The primary motive behind every fight for independence is to be able to stand alone, make decisions without any external influence, be free of the control of others, and live life the way they think it should be lived. This makes independence sound like a sure deal for good living.

The longing for independence usually occurs when a relationship goes sour. The suffering party will seek to opt out and be left alone—as they should. That's what happens in codependent relationships and other forms of toxic relationship. In this book, I've discussed some steps you need to take to end and recover from toxic relationships, especially those involving codependency and narcissism. But the essence of taking you through that process isn't to lead you into another cycle of problems. Everything I've shared in this book to this point is to ensure you're free from toxicity. It's to liberate you from every emotional disorder that comes with toxic relationships. Most importantly, it's to lead you to be *free*.

Independence is a great thing to seek. A parallel can be drawn between codependency and independence; they're two ends of the relationship spectrum that can never blend. In codependency, you're obsessed with looking out for your partner, so much so that you allow their lifestyle to influence your emotions, attitudes, and behavior. In the process, you forget to take care of yourself because you believe that your self-worth comes from what you do for your partner. But independence is different. It's a phase in a relationship that's higher and better than codependency.

In an independent relationship, you don't feel responsible for what happens to the other person. You allow them to live their life while you live yours without remorse or guilt. As an independent partner, you're self-reliant and self-empowered. Your emotional, physical, and spiritual needs are your sole responsibility. You pride yourself on your ability to make independent choices and do things your way. And that's where your self-worth and self-esteem emanate from.

In recovering from a toxic relationship, independence is a comfortable haven to go to first. The reason to set healthy boundaries and be assertive in your decisions is so that you can be free from the control of the other person in the relationship. It's the same reason a colony fights to stand alone, to be able to self-govern the affairs of its domain. That's the first thing you need to learn to do as well. Your life is precious, and the person you'll eventually become hinges on the decisions you make about your relationships.

This book has been designed to equip you to make the right decisions for yourself. I've discussed the intricacies of toxic relationships and how to end them in the first two parts. If you've followed the book to this point, you'll know that you don't need someone else to steer your life anymore. Hopefully, you've begun to realize that it's time for you to take the reins and drive. That's being independent.

How to Become More Confident and Independent

One of the things that happened while you were in a toxic relationship is that your self-confidence was battered. But if you've gotten to this recovery phase, you'll need your confidence back to live life to the fullest.

Confidence comes as a result of a variety of factors. It's not one size fits all. Different people derive confidence from different things, but according to Bridges (2017), choices and accomplishments that make you feel happy and proud of who you are generally make great confidence boosters.

Here are a few things you can do to boost your self-confidence, independently:

Find Activities That Give You a Sense of Fulfillment

There's a feeling of happiness you get from doing things you like to do. For instance, I derive joy from sitting down at my laptop to write. It makes me happy that I can string words together to pass a concise message to people. I love to cook, too, even though I don't cook very often. Whenever I cook, I get this sense of satisfaction from it. That feeling of, "Boy, you just prepared a great meal" makes my heart leap for joy. The fulfillment derived from this accomplishment makes me eager to tell guests, "I cooked this meal."

Whatever you're interested in—a hobby, a passion, even chores—discover it and indulge yourself in doing it as frequently as you can. It'll help to add blocks of strength to your growing confidence.

Create a Daily Personal To-Do List

I've also tried this, and I recommend it to people as well. It has really helped me and those I've recommended it to. Think of everything you need to do today and write a list (you can write it on paper, a sticky note, or your phone). Let that list guide your day. Let it be your compass for engaging with the day, and ensure that regardless of the distractions you encounter, you stick to the items on the list.

There's usually a sense of accomplishment to be gained from ticking off each completed task. It makes you feel good about yourself, and it raises your level of confidence in accomplishing anything you set your heart on doing.

This is important: Don't just *think* about what you want to do today—*write it down*. It might come to you as a thought, but you need to be diligent enough to write it in a place where you can see it and tick it off. This creates a positive psychological effect.

Also, don't beat yourself up if, at the end of the day, you haven't completed a task on the list. A lot of things can come up during the day which may inhibit you from finishing the task. Just think of how you can make up for it tomorrow.

Be Committed to Making Wise Choices

Some time ago, I made a financial decision that didn't seem logical at the time. I committed myself to consistently saving a percentage of my income. I ensured I was faithful in doing so. It didn't make any sense at the time, but as I kept at it, I became proud of that habit—and it turned out to be one of the best financial decisions I ever made. I was so excited about it that I'm now confident enough to share it with just about anyone when the need arises. Making that choice increased my confidence in talking about financial management.

In the same vein, make a commitment to yourself to make wise career choices. Take a professional course. Plan to upskill. Make plans to attend conferences, workshops, and/or seminars. These are the kinds of choices that will boost your confidence. Make choices that'll make you a better partner, friend, leader, or colleague.

Exercise

Bridges (2017) notes that exercise isn't just for building a good physique and healthy body; it's also beneficial for memory retention, focus, stress management and preventing depression. With this in mind, create time in your daily schedule to exercise. Don't aim for perfection; the goal is to make small changes in your physical health that help you build your self-confidence.

Step Out of Your Comfort Zone

This strategy could be tough to apply, but it's one of the most effective ways of boosting your confidence.

What do you dread doing? Whatever it is, plan to give it a try. For instance, if you've never traveled far away from home and you feel a bit nervous about the idea—book a trip. Perhaps you've always dreaded the idea of hiking—why not try it out?

Once you're able to face your fears and you accomplish something, the confidence that comes with the exclamation of, "Yeah! I did it!" is always amazing. It can strengthen your confidence, and you may realize that avoiding that thing has been limiting your potential and fulfillment.

When you step out of your comfort zone, you might be setting yourself up for opportunities you've missed in the past. It could set you up for new business partnerships, relationships, client acquisitions, scholarships, etc.

Focus on Your Strength

The more you concentrate on the things you can't do, the more you'll feel bad about yourself. Learn to accept that there are some things you can't do; perhaps you just aren't wired for them, or perhaps you don't have the skills required to do those things at the moment. Don't beat yourself up about it. Instead, focus on what you *do* have the capability to do.

There are things you're exceptionally good at. Funnily enough, when people focus all their energy on the things they can't do, they tend to forget all about their potential. You're gifted. You might not be able to do certain things, but there are other things you can do. Concentrate your energy on those things.

Stop focusing on your errors. Celebrate your achievements and let them spur you on to work on the weak spots.

Stop Comparing Yourself

Comparison is an easy way to tank your confidence, especially when you focus more on the accomplishments of the other person and on your own failures.

Stop it! You're deflating your confidence.

Don't focus on other people's achievements—focus on your path. Of course, you could learn from the success stories of others, but don't use them as your yardstick for measuring your own success.

Balancing Independence with Interdependence

When you're recovering from a toxic relationship, especially a romantic relationship, one of the things we've discussed that you need to learn is how to set healthy boundaries. This will help you to regain your freedom and take charge of your life once again.

If you're in a situation where you don't have to leave the relationship but you need to stop being codependent, setting boundaries will allow you to live an independent lifestyle in that relationship. You won't need to depend on your partner for validation or to build your self-worth. You won't need the input of other people to make certain decisions; you'll be able to independently make those choices yourself. You won't feel responsible for anyone's life, and you'll focus on living your own life and pursuing your dreams.

Basically, you'll be able to say good riddance to toxicity. Sounds amazing, right? Yes, I agree—it is!

But let's look at the flip side of this coin:

In our society, we often view independence as an indication of being afraid to depend on other people (Khurana, 2017). The fear of being controlled or manipulated by others is the primary motivation for seeking independence. According to Khurana (2017), true independence doesn't mean simply freeing yourself from the yokes of all relationships, dusting your hands of all social responsibilities, and doing whatever you want without taking others into account whatsoever.

If independence is taken to the extreme in this way, a few things that will likely happen to your relationship include:

- Emotional detachment
- Declining communication
- Apathy
- Eventual death of the relationship

Independence is great, but there's a higher level of relationship you should know about. It's *interdependency*. Independence is not the ultimate goal. It's actually not the best kind of relationship—the kind that can guarantee lasting peace and joy.

Interdependence opens the possibility of bringing down your walls so that other people can access your true feelings and opinions. This should be done respectfully, without the other person trampling on you while you're vulnerable. Opening up to others enables you to be available for your partner to attend to their physical, emotional, and spiritual needs, while they also attend to yours, too. Interdependence is not a one-sided affair, but a mutual commitment.

Overcoming Barriers to Interdependence

Let's look at how a fundamental misunderstanding of the function of independence in a relationship can lead to problems.

Amanda and her husband, Mike, had been married for five years, and they both claimed that they were independent. They were happy that they had different careers and separate friend circles. However, Amanda sometimes got annoyed when Mike forgot about their plans to do things together. Instead of expressing how she felt to her husband, she would let off steam through other channels; she didn't want anyone to think of her as being "needy" or "weak." Whenever she wasn't happy with Mike's behavior, she threw herself into her work or talked to her friends to distract herself from the irritation.

Mike, on his end, didn't create time for Amanda either. He was always at work. After all, he was independent, right? Eventually, Amanda felt Mike was making his work his top priority while she came second. She started to feel insecure, but she still didn't tell him.

Soon afterwards, Amanda got pregnant. Mike was supposed to meet her at the doctor's office, but at the last minute he called her to say he would be late because he wanted to finish up a task at the office. And that was it! Amanda's temper flared. She called her husband a selfish person. Mike didn't understand why she was angry, and that made Amanda even angrier.

As you can see, complete independence doesn't really work out in relationships. Truth is, nature designed humans to function interdependently, not independently. You may have had a toxic relationship at some point, but that doesn't mean the next step for you is to live independently—not relating with anyone—for the rest of your life. You still need a network of relationships around you.

It's when people don't understand the true essence of independence that they take it to the extreme. Thus, the balance to our understanding of independence is knowing that the order of things in nature is interdependence: a mutual relationship, in spite of our individuality.

Interdependence doesn't rob you of your freedom or independence, it enhances it. While independence will make you a great individual boxer, single tennis player, or soloist, interdependence will make you an amazing football captain or team player. For the vast majority of things in life, we need to work with other people to achieve our goals.

But a lot of people still don't understand interdependence, and that constitutes one of the barriers to practicing interdependence. How do we remove these barriers?

Step out of your cocoon: You need to realize that you can't get too far in achieving your dreams when you're alone. So step out and embrace the possibility of a partnership.

Be open to talking: Good communication is one of the key elements of an interdependent relationship. Don't assume that your partner knows something. Talk about it. Talk about everything and hide nothing, including your grievances.

Create time to be with them: Being independent means that you have to build boundaries for your own benefits. But to enjoy a healthy, mutual relationship, you'll need to lower the fence and create specific times to interact with your partner. Don't shut them out totally. Now that you understand your individuality, you can spend better quality time with them.

Respect their boundaries: Just as you want other people to respect your boundaries, you should also respect theirs. If not, you'll step on each other's toes. The outcome won't be great.

Be sincere: Don't be suspicious of your partner. Trust is one of the most crucial characteristics of an interdependent relationship. If you're suspicious or distrusting of your partner, you'll create an environment for toxicity.

Please note that the knowledge you've gained about toxic relationships and the signs of each type should be able to guide you in avoiding getting into another one. It'll also prevent you from losing your individuality as you embark on an interdependent relationship.

Celebrating Independence

How is interdependence better than codependency? Write down three ways.

_____

_____

_____

_____

It is important to know the things that keep us busy and give us great joy. Trying new things also allows us to discover activities that can help reduce our tendency towards codependence.

Write down five activities that give you a sense of fulfillment.

Activity 1:

_____

_____

Activity 2:

_____

_____

Activity 3:

_____

Activity 4:

_____

_____

Activity 5:

_____

_____

Why haven't you been able to do some of those activities that give you joy and fulfillment?

_____

_____

_____

_____

Which of the following have you done recently?

    A. Attended a conference or workshop

    B. Been on an excursion

    C. Gone on a road trip

    D. Exercised

    E. Attended a concert

    F. Visited an art gallery

Create a bucket list of things you're going to do (by yourself) before this year is over. Write those activities in the list below and set a date for them.

BUCKET LIST

☐ ....

☐ ....

☐ ....

☐ ....

BUCKET LIST

☐ ....

☐ ....

☐ ....

☐ ....

BUCKET LIST

- ☐ ....
- ☐ ....
- ☐ ....
- ☐ ....

BUCKET LIST

- ☐ ....
- ☐ ....
- ☐ ....
- ☐ ....

P.S. Learning to be independent is a major way to stop codependency. It helps if you can learn to enjoy life and do what makes you happy without depending on someone else or waiting for their permission.

Chapter Seven Takeaway

Healthy relationships are rare gifts. Such relationships create the right environment for us to become all the amazing things we've been created to be. We cannot afford to lose such relationships.

To keep these healthy relationships, do the following:

- Don't make a fuss about tiny issues
- Communicate with clarity
- Avoid assumptions
- Don't shy away from arguments—have healthy, respectful ones
- Always pay attention to the bright side of things
- Admit that your relationship is not immune to challenges
- Learn and practice trust
- Prioritize each other
- Be each other's biggest fan
- Respect your individualities

Interdependence is possible, and you can merge it with independence. You need people; people need you. It's a two-way street. Get that balance right and you'll be well on your way to healthy, happy relationships. You know I wouldn't mess with you—it really is that simple.

CHAPTER EIGHT

The Radical Self-Love Guide and Workbook

"You shall love your neighbor as yourself."

—Mark 12:31 (NKJV)

"The absence of self-love can never be replaced with the presence of people's love for you."

— Edmond Mbiaka

What Is Self-Love?

In an article for *Cosmopolitan*, actress Raveena Tandon shares the story of her two-decade journey to body acceptance. From the early years of her life, she had a love-hate relationship with her body. She hated herself as a young girl because she was overweight and everyone in her class teased her for it. Despite this, she went on to start her acting career at age 16. Her body was the same size, but in the early years of her career, she didn't feel insecure. Then the media came along, labeling and body-shaming her on a regular basis. Female journalists were the leader of the pack. They labeled her "Miss Thunder Thighs" and "Amazonian." These comments made her extremely conscious of her body.

Raveena is a tall woman with a big build. Since she wasn't slim, she tried to find clothes that suited her body type. Even as a public figure, she struggled to accept her body. The struggle continued in her twenties and thirties. It was until her forties that she began to feel comfortable with the way she was. She started dressing more confidently and resolved to focus on being a confident woman instead of trying to fit someone else's idea of a "perfect" body.

As Raveena discovered, loving yourself is the best thing you can do for yourself. This is regardless of your background, status, or age. There's no universal definition of what self-love is, but you can figure out whether you love yourself or not through reading these descriptions.

Martin (2019) and Borenstein (2020) each give a long list of descriptions of self-love. You love yourself if you:

- Always talk to yourself with love
- Always talk about yourself with love
- Forgive yourself every time you mess up
- Commit to meeting your own needs

- Take a break from self-judgment
- Are assertive
- Trust yourself
- Recognize your strengths
- Are true to yourself
- Value your feelings
- Are nice to yourself
- Prioritize your health and total wellbeing
- Set healthy boundaries
- Challenge yourself to be better
- Pursue your interests and goals
- Say positive things to yourself
- Accept your imperfections
- Spend time with the people who support you and believe in you
- Avoid toxic people
- Ask for help
- Make healthy choices most times
- Don't let other people take advantage of you
- Live according to your set values and principles
- Hold yourself accountable
- Release grudges or anger that holds you back

- Set realistic expectations
- Appreciate your effort to become a better version of yourself
- Notice and celebrate your progress
- Give yourself healthy treats

This list isn't exhaustive. There are many more. However, this description will give you a glimpse of what self-love means and allow you to assess yourself with it. You're beautiful only if you see yourself as beautiful. You're smart only if you regard yourself as smart. Whatever the quality or characteristic, you're a product of the way you see yourself. Your self-worth, self-esteem, and self-confidence hinge on your love for self.

Debunking Self-Love Myths

From my interactions with different people, I've realized that everyone has their own idea of what self-love is, but in truth, it's not what they think. In this section, I'll share a few misconceptions and try to show you the true side of it as well.

Myth 1: Self-love is self-centered

Self-love could sound like you're only focused on yourself without minding what goes on with other people. It could also sound like you're only taking care of yourself, but that's not what it's all about.

If self-love is viewed from the standpoint that you're better and more worthy than other people, you'll lose the moral heart to extend love to the people around you. The real essence of self-love is to embrace yourself with great compassion and earnest faith in yourself. And while doing so, you extend the same compassion to others as well.

In essence, self-love starts with you but it doesn't end with you. It makes you a better human with whom others can have a healthy relationship.

Myth 2: Self-love is a path to self-sufficiency

No! It's true that to love yourself properly, you need to set healthy boundaries. And such boundaries limit the access some folks have to you. It stands as a wall that wards off toxic people.

However, you should also remember what I told you about interdependence. To believe that self-love leads to self-sufficiency is to defy the law of nature. No one is self-sufficient. We need people around us in different contexts at different times. We cannot reach our goals alone. Any description of self-love that contradicts the principle of interdependence is wrong. Self-love makes you an independent individual who can have better relationships with other people without being intimidated into conforming to other people's opinions.

Myth 3: Self-love makes you complacent

When describing self-love to people, we tell them to take their eyes off their weaknesses, flaws, and mistakes and focus on their strengths. But we're not saying you should ignore your mistakes and never take responsibility for your life.

Self-love doesn't mean being irresponsible; in fact, it makes you take charge of your life and live your life to the fullest. You can't do that if you're complacent and you leave things to fate. Self-love doesn't mean that you should accept your flaws and say things like, "Well, that's just the way I am. I love myself this way. There's nothing I can do about it." It's actually quite the opposite—if you love yourself, you'll work on getting better. There's no form of work that's done complacently. It all requires a certain degree of diligence and commitment.

Myth 4: Self-love is about proving a point to other people

What point do you want to prove by loving yourself? The only person you need to prove anything to is yourself. That's what self-love is. Over the years, people have told you that you can't do certain things and you believed them. You tell yourself you can't do it, too. You refuse to attempt anything worthwhile because you've failed at it once. The only person affected here is you—your self-esteem, self-worth, and self-confidence have been shattered.

When you begin to love yourself properly, you'll tell yourself that you can do what people said you couldn't. You can succeed in the things you've failed at before. You're pushing yourself to believe in possibilities. That's how to love yourself.

Will people see your progress and evolution? Of course! Nothing good can be hidden for too long. But your real intention for doing the amazing things you do for yourself isn't to make a statement or prove a point to anyone.

Myth 5: Self-love is only for those who struggle to believe in themselves

As much as this may sound true, it doesn't reveal the whole truth about the practice of self-love.

Although people who are experiencing an identity crisis or relationship problems might need it more than other people who feel confident in themselves, we all need to love ourselves unconditionally. Life isn't a bed of roses. There are days when life will toss challenges our way. The way we handle those challenges shows how much we've invested in our minds. Anyone who doesn't love themselves lives by chance, but those who love themselves and want to continue on the path of success invest in themselves and enrich themselves mentally, spiritually, and physically. You don't need to have an identity or relationship crisis to love yourself.

Myth 6: Self-love says all you need to excel is within you

Self-love teaches you to look within and appreciate the great gifts you've been endowed with, but it certainly doesn't teach you that all that's within you is sufficient to take you to your destination. Your innate abilities are enough to sustain you, but self-love also teaches you to recognize the gifts in others and appreciate them for the things they contribute to your existence and the existence of the human race.

The most important thing to remember about self-love is that you're living from the inside out. This means that if you're healthy within, you can have healthy relationships with other people. If you love yourself, you can give the same love to others.

How to Start Loving Yourself

Now that you know what self-love is and what it's not, the next most pertinent question is: How do I start loving myself? Self-love may come in the form of eating healthy, exercising, or having healthy relationships.

Here are a few ways you can start:

Be committed: The best way to start learning how to love yourself is to commit yourself to doing so. It must be an intentional learning process. The results might not come as quickly as you want, but your commitment to learning will keep you at it until you begin to get the desired result.

Control your impulses: Our impulses and desires can be weird at times. For instance, there are times we crave certain foods. If we respond to and overindulge in our desires, the aftermath of such a response is that a feeling of condemnation washes over us. To start practicing self-love, you must learn to distinguish between the things you need and the things you want. Focus on the things you need only. Reduce the control your impulsive desires have over you.

Practice healthy habits: Decide within yourself to practice healthy habits like eating right and exercising. Commit to doing valuable things during the day, spend time with your family, have healthy conversations with friends and colleagues, etc. Don't do these things out of compulsion or necessity; do them because you want to.

Be patient: Don't expect these things to begin to yield immediate results. If you're coming from a point where you don't treat yourself well enough, you'll need time to adjust and adapt to this new learning scheme. Therefore, be patient with yourself. Just as a baby learns to walk, learn to take one step at a time. Don't be in haste to become perfect at once. Love is patient.

Have dialogues with yourself: It helps a lot if you can create time to have honest conversations with yourself. This could look like a moment of reflection or self-evaluation. The most important thing is that you're questioning beliefs you have perhaps held for years and have allowed to define you.

Ask yourself about your values, beliefs, emotions, behavioral patterns, habits, etc. The things you find out will help you to make necessary adjustments to begin to live right.

The benefits that come with loving yourself are enormous. It will improve everything in your life—your self-esteem, relationships, self-worth, self-confidence, health, and wellbeing. Fulfilling your dreams will become possible.

A Special Note: What Does the Bible Say about Codependency?

God created man and all other creatures to function in perfect harmony. God's structure of creation was simple: man would be in control of the entirety of creation, while everything would work together for man (Genesis 1:26-30). At another time, God created a helper for the man because of the nature of his tasks (Genesis 2:18).

This shows that God's template for the whole of creation was interdependence. God intended the world to function by mutual relationship.

Unfortunately, after the great fall (Genesis 3:1-19), man became an arrogant, self-seeking, deceptive, and murderous being (Genesis 4:3-10) who would do anything to preserve his ego and remain the center of attention. That was the beginning of toxic relationships according to these scriptural records.

Jesus the True Model

Jesus had a great relationship with His disciples. The force behind all His actions was love. As a leader, He demonstrated love for all of humanity by releasing himself to be punished and sacrificed on behalf of the entire human race. This makes sacrifice the highest form of demonstrating love.

Contemporary Christians

Two millennia after the departure of Jesus, contemporary Christians are still expected to follow in the footsteps of Jesus–to walk in love (Ephesians 5:2). But Jesus made it clear that the extent to which you love your neighbor shows the extent to which you love yourself (Mark 12:31).

Love is the sole law that guides the Christian community. But what does this love mean? Going by the example in the Bible:

- Love is sacrifice (John 15:13)
- Love is selfless service (Matthew 20:26-27)
- Love is giving (John 3:16)
- Love is genuine interest in others (Philippians 2:4)

Does This Love Make Me Foolish?

Love is not foolish. A lot of Christians misunderstand what it means to love genuinely. But gleaning wisdom from the life of Jesus will show the truth. If love is patient and kind, then Jesus, being the perfect example of a lover, was patient and kind. But despite His patience and kindness, He never allowed anyone to take advantage of Him. He went wherever He chose to go, not where the people wanted Him (Mark 1:37-38). He visited the places He wanted to visit whether people approved of it or not (Luke 19:1-10). He was in charge of His life.

Love makes you compassionate, but you shouldn't run into debt because you're trying to help another Christian. We have been exhorted to bear each other's burden (Galatians 6:2), but how can you bear another's burden when your own needs your attention?

Ultimately, to sacrifice something valuable for someone in the name of love has to be by choice, not out of self-pity. Jesus said that He laid down His life willingly; He wasn't compelled to do so (John 10:18). He was an independent leader who didn't derive His sense of fulfillment from doing what people would have Him do, but from doing whatever He knew was best for Himself and others.

A Closing Statement

In closing, self-love is not about shutting yourself out of the world while you create a utopic space for yourself alone, a space where all that matters is you. Rather, it's an opportunity to create a healthy and serene space within in order to accommodate new relationships. It's a powerful way of finding your feet again and walking on the path of fulfillment. And as you do so, you release the fragrance of love to those you meet on your path.

Workbook Eight
Exercise One

Fill in the blanks with words of self-love showing who you are and what you now believe about yourself. For example, "I am intelligent."

1. I am

_____

2. I am

_____

3. I am

_____

4. I am

_____

5. I am

_____

6. I am

_____

7. I am

_____

8. I am

_____

9. I am

_____

10. I am

_____

How you view yourself matters. All these words you've written about yourself aren't mere writing exercises. Read them aloud daily, and you'll see how much more you'll begin to respect yourself and fall in love with your being.

Exercise Two

This activity will help you ascertain things you love and hate about yourself. When you're done filling in the boxes, work on the things you hate about yourself. This will help you have more things you love about yourself. The more things you have on your love list, the more you'll love yourself.

WHAT YOU LOVE ABOUT YOURSELF	WHAT YOU HATE ABOUT YOURSELF

Chapter Eight Takeaway

A popular disinfectant brand that I love has a slogan along these lines: "If I don't take care of you, who will?"

Well, let's invert that now, shall we? If you don't take care of yourself, who will?

Take care of yourself. You get the drift.

Conclusion

My husband and I were married for 16 years and had two beautiful daughters. Our lives couldn't have been better. Until they got worse. He met a woman at the gym, and I was suddenly "too old." When he served me divorce papers, I thought I was in a nightmare. My life fell apart in two weeks as one thing led to another and we finalized the divorce. I thought I would die.

I'm telling this story now, five years later, and I'm fine because I've moved on. What I want to share is this: My happiness now is not automatic. I'm happy because I'm doing well for myself, and also because I've got wonderful people around me who support me.

If one human makes you sad, another human will make you happy. If you had a toxic relationship, you can have a new, non-toxic one. If you were codependent and had to break free, you can become interdependent and begin to love healthily. You need people, even if you've been hurt by humans in the past.

—Story by Serena

As early as the late third century AD, there was a group of individuals—men and women—who lived in different times and places in history, but had similar experiences. Common to their experiences is the fact that they all wanted to attain a higher level of spiritual perfection. They wanted to be morally upright and holy. Therefore, they committed themselves to asceticism. Some took their practice to the extreme; they isolated themselves from civilization and people and began living alone in the ancient Egyptian deserts. They're known as "desert fathers and mothers."

Although a few of them achieved their goals, this is not the best path forward for most people in this modern age. Humans might be flawed and damaged, but how can we live out our dreams and explore our potential if we're not living in this flawed space together as a society?

You may have had some nasty experiences in your relationships, and that could be one of the main reasons you chose to read this book. But your past experience doesn't change the fact that you still need to live your life in the human community. The question, then, is: How do you live in a society filled with all different kinds of humans and still be fulfilled and happy?

That's one of the questions to which I hope this book has provided a robust answer. Primarily, my aim with this book has been to focus on specific types of relationships: those that are toxic and dangerous for your wellbeing. Having interacted with a lot of people, I can confidently say that codependency and narcissism are both toxic in relationships, and many people are silently suffering in their relationships as a result.

Being in such a relationship is proof that humans are still flawed, including you—but the good news is that humans can change and become better. We can all become better partners, live happily with our family members, and have healthy work relationships with our colleagues at the office.

This book has offered practical steps to help anyone who seeks to become a better human. I didn't stop there, though. The first port of call is to become an independent individual who doesn't need to depend on others to live a good life. One of the things a toxic relationship does is make you dependent on someone else's evaluation of you (often, these are demeaning and devastating evaluations that make you feel bad and even, in some cases, unworthy of living).

When you take the steps I've shown in this book, you'll begin to realize that there's more to life than what someone you were in a relationship with has told you. Therefore, having an independent opinion of yourself is the first step to becoming a better human.

However, to have a good opinion of yourself, you need to love yourself unapologetically. It's only then you'll be able to wash off the negative labels and toxic perspectives you've held about yourself due to what others have said.

Being an independent individual in relationships is only the start of your journey to becoming a better human in society. You'll still need other people to live a fulfilled life; no one is self-sufficient. You need other people—healthy people—in your circle. In this way, you'll achieve a higher level of relationship whereby you retain your individuality, but you're still a great partner, and you enjoy your life to the fullest.

I trust that this book has taken you on a journey of self-realization, healing, and recovery. From the first page to the last, I hope there have been moments of truth and revelation. I know you're ready for a change. It's your time to face that fear. You're ready to meet the new you.

So, don't hesitate—go start applying everything you've learned so far, if you haven't already.

Finally, if you've gotten answers to your questions from this book, and it's been helping you to become a better person, please leave a review on Amazon so other amazing people like you can start their own journey to become better humans too.

Thank You

Thank you so much for purchasing my book.

You could have picked from dozens of other books, but you took a chance and chose this one.

So, THANK YOU SO MUCH for getting this book and for making it all the way to the end.

Before you go, I wanted to ask you for one small favor. **Could you please consider writing a review on Amazon? Posting a review is the best and easiest way to help other people gain true freedom from codependency.**

Let's do this together! Your review will help other people discover the information in this book, and your feedback will help me to keep writing the kinds of books that will help you get the results you want. I would love to hear from you.

Leave a review on Amazon US. SCAN with your camera

Leave a review on Amazon UK. SCAN with your camera

References

Beattie, M. (1992). *Codependent no more: How to stop controlling others and start caring for yourself.* Center City, MN: Hazelden.

Blais, S. (2020). *How childhood trauma has influenced my love life.* Medium. Retrieved from https://medium.com/age-of-awareness/how-childhood-trauma-has-affected-my-love-life-44b6a3d0b463

Borenstein, J. (2020). *Self-love and what it means.* Brain & Behavior Research Foundation. Retrieved from https://www.bbrfoundation.org/blog/self-love-and-what-it-means

Brenneman, C. (2016). *3 strategies to balance selfish and selfless.* The Spaniard. Retrieved from https://www.charliespaniard.com/3-strategies-balance-selfish-selfless/

Bridges, F. (2017). *10 ways to build confidence.* Forbes. Retrieved from https://www.forbes.com/sites/francesbridges/2017/07/21/10-ways-to-build-confidence/?sh=3fb5668d3c59

Carmichael, S. G. (2015). *The research is clear: Long hours backfire for people and for companies.* Harvard Business

Review. Retrieved from https://hbr.org/2015/08/the-research-is-clear-long-hours-backfire-for-people-and-for-companies

Carter, C. M. (2022). *Stopping the need to be needed: How to avoid codependency in parenting.* Motherly. Retrieved from https://www.mother.ly/parenting/codependent-parent/

Cory, T. L. (2022). *What is a toxic relationship? – 8 signs of toxic relationships.* Health Scope Magazine. Retrieved from https://healthscopemag.com/health-scope/toxic-relationships/

Coursera (2023). *Assertive communication: How to do it (and why it matters).* Retrieved from https://www.coursera.org/articles/assertive-communication

Cox, J. (2022). *How to recover from narcissistic abuse.* Psych Central. Retrieved from https://psychcentral.com/disorders/narcissistic-personality-disorder/narcissistic-abuse-recovery-healing-from-the-discard

Daya Houston. (2020). *Dealing with narcissistic abuse - a true story.* Blog. Retrieved from https://www.dayahouston.org/post/dealing-with-narcissistic-abuse-a-true-story

Del Russo, M. (2017). *The difference between a "healthy" & an "unhealthy" argument.* Refinery29. Retrieved from https://www.refinery29.com/en-us/couple-healthy-vs-unhealthy-arguments

Gilbert, B. (2020). *Do you have a codependent personality?* Everyday Health. Retrieved from https://www.everydayhealth.com/emotional-health/do-you-have-a-codependent-personality.aspx

Gonsalves, K. (2022). *The 4 attachment styles in relationships + how to find yours.* MindBodyGreen. Retrieved from https://www.mindbodygreen.com/articles/attachment-theory-and-the-4-attachment-styles

Hagar, K. (2023). *Being selfish vs being selfless, how to find the balance.* UpJourney. Retrieved from https://upjourney.com/being-selfish-vs-being-selfless-how-to-find-the-balance

Herman, K. (2021). *Six self-care tips on overcoming abuse-related trauma.* Nami. Retrieved from https://www.nami.org/Blogs/NAMI-Blog/January-2021/Six-Self-Care-Tips-on-Overcoming-Abuse-Related-Trauma

Khurana, U. (2017). *Independence vs interdependence.* LinkedIn. Retrieved from https://www.linkedin.com/pulse/independence-vs-interdependence-udit-khurana/

Lewis, R. (2020). *Types of attachment styles and what they mean.* Healthline. Retrieved from https://www.healthline.com/health/parenting/types-of-attachment

Lewis, R. (2020). *8 signs that you might be a codependent parent — and how to heal.* Healthline. Retrieved from https://www.healthline.com/health/parenting/parent-codependency

Mackel, S. (2018). *Codependency: A dysfunctional love story.* The Focus on You. Retrieved from http://thefocusonyou.com/codependency-love-story/

Martin, S. (2016). *How to deal with people who repeatedly violate your boundaries.* Psych Central. Retrieved from https://psychcentral.com/blog/imperfect/2016/07/how-to-deal-with-people-who-repeatedly-violate-your-boundaries

Martin S. (2019). *What is self-love and why is it so important?* Psych Central. Retrieved from https://psychcentral.com/blog/imperfect/2019/05/what-is-self-love-and-why-is-it-so-important

Mayo Clinic Staff (n.d.) *Stress management.* Mayo Clinic. Retrieved from https://www.mayoclinic.org/healthy-lifestyle/stress-management/in-depth/assertive/art-20044644

Michail, J. (2020). *Strong nonverbal skills matter now more than ever in this "new normal."* Forbes. Retrieved from https://www.forbes.com/sites/forbescoachescouncil/2020/

08/24/strong-nonverbal-skills-matter-now-more-than-ever-in-this-new-normal

Neuharth, D. (2017). *14 thought-control tactics narcissists use to confuse and dominate you.* Psych Central. Retrieved from https://psychcentral.com/blog/narcissism-decoded/2017/09/14-thought-control-tactics-narcissists-use-to-confuse-and-dominate-you

The NIV Bible. (n.d.). *Martha the people pleaser.* NIV Bible Blog. Retrieved from https://www.thenivbible.com/blog/a-the-people-pleaser/

Pablo, S. (2021). *Being selfish vs being selfless, how to find the balance.* UpJourney. Retrieved from https://upjourney.com/being-selfish-vs-being-selfless-how-to-find-the-balance

Papayanis, A. (2021). *Confessions of a recovering 'people pleaser.'* Huffington Post. Retrieved from https://www.huffpost.com/entry/people-pleaser-how-to-stop_n_61786fc8e4b0657357419f73

Regan, S. (2022). *9 signs of a toxic family & how to deal with it, from therapists.* MindBodyGreen. Retrieved from https://www.mindbodygreen.com/articles/toxic-families

Scott, E. (2022). *What is a toxic relationship? How to spot the warning signs of toxic relationships.* VeryWell Mind. Retrieved from https://www.verywellmind.com/toxic-relationships-4174665

Sherwood, M. (2021). *Being selfish vs being selfless, how to find the balance.* UpJourney. Retrieved from https://upjourney.com/being-selfish-vs-being-selfless-how-to-find-the-balance

SUN Behavioral Health. (n.d.). *The causes of codependency.* Blog. Retrieved from https://sundelaware.com/the-causes-of-codependency/

Sutton, J. (2021). *How to perform assertiveness skills training: 6 exercises.* Positive Psychology. Retrieved from https://positivepsychology.com/assertiveness-training/

Thomas, S. (2016). *Healing from hidden abuse: A journey through the stages of recovery from psychological abuse.* New York: MAST Publishing House.

Thum, M. (2013). *Walking the fine line between compassion and asserting yourself.* Myrko Thum. Retrieved from https://www.myrkothum.com/compassion-and-assertion/

Williams, P. (2021). *5 differences between people-pleasing and authentic kindness.* Medium. Retrieved from https://medium.com/change-your-mind/5-differences-between-people-pleasing-and-authentic-kindness-4b50d31a53f2

Wyeth, S. (2015). *Two opposing skills no leader can do without: Find the best balance between being assertive and being empathetic.* Inc. Africa. Retrieved from https://incafrica.com/library/sims-wyeth-two-opposing-skills-no-leader-can-do-without

Other Sources

https://www.goodreads.com/work/quotes/59440924-the-art-of-everyday-assertiveness-speak-up-say-no-set-boundaries-tak

https://www.goodreads.com/quotes/tag/people-pleasing

https://www.goodreads.com/quotes/tag/toxic-relationships

https://www.cosmopolitan.in/celebrity/features/g21601/10-women-share-their-inspiring-self-love-stories

https://loveandlifetoolbox.com/too-independent-in-your-relationship/

https://www.brainyquote.com/quotes/henry_van_dyke_1473 11?src=t_interdependence

https://www.goodhousekeeping.com/life/g38333580/self-love-quotes/

https://www.goodreads.com/work/quotes/86406480-narcissistic-abuse-and-codependency-a-step-by-step-guide-to-dealing-wit

https://www.goodreads.com/quotes/tag/attachment-theory

Made in the USA
Las Vegas, NV
15 August 2023

76154921R00114